Living the Psalms

Banner Mini Guides introduce the reader to some of the major themes and issues related to the Christian faith. They lay a solid foundation of Bible teaching while encouraging more thorough exploration of the theme with suggestions for further reading. The mini-guides will seamlessly fit into the teaching quarters of the church year with their thirteen-chapter format, making them useful for group as well as for individual study.

Living the Psalms

Learning to Glorify and Enjoy God Each Day

Banner Mini-Guides

Christian Living

David P. Murray

THE BANNER OF TRUTH TRUST

THE BANNER OF TRUTH TRUST

Head Office
3 Murrayfield Road
Edinburgh, EH12 6EL
UK

North America Office
610 Alexander Spring Road
Carlisle, PA 17015
USA

banneroftruth.org

ISBN
Print: 978 1 80040 367 3
Epub: 978 1 80040 368 0
Kindle: 978 1 80040 369 7

*

Typeset in 10/14 pt Minion Pro
at the Banner of Truth Trust, Edinburgh

Printed in the USA by
Versa Press, Inc.,
East Peoria, IL

To
JORDAN NIKKEL
who has taught me more than anyone
how to worship God in spirit and in truth.

Contents

Introduction

When a famous singer dies, his or her relatives often find previously unreleased songs among their possessions. The family or friends will often produce an album of these songs, and mourning fans, who had resigned themselves to never hearing any more new songs from their idol, rush to buy this unexpected bonus material.

What would you say if I told you that I'd found previously unheard songs of Jesus? Songs about him that he composed and sang? Wouldn't you rush out to buy them and hear them? Wouldn't you want to learn how to sing them too?

Well, here's the strange thing, you don't need to buy them, because you already have them. But you probably hardly know them. Or you may know some of them, but you never realized that they were actually songs about Jesus, co-written by Jesus,[1] and sung by Jesus.

I'm talking about the Psalms, and the purpose of this short book is to help you discover these bonus songs and

---

[1] When I say 'co-written by Jesus,' what I mean is that Jesus inspired human penmen to write the Psalms. The Spirit of Christ was in them when they wrote these songs (see 1 Pet. 1:11; 2 Tim. 3:16, 17). Jesus, therefore, is the ultimate author, but he worked through human authors.

sing them as you've never sung them before. Although composed a thousand years before Jesus lived on earth as a man, I want to show you that these songs were co-written by Jesus, are about Jesus, and were sung by Jesus when he came to live in our world. Who wouldn't want to learn how to sing such songs?

Now I realize there are some objections to viewing the Psalms in this way, and singing the Psalms as part of our Christian life and worship. That's why I begin this mini-guide by answering these objections and by highlighting many of the spiritual benefits of singing them.

To keep in tune with the practical nature of the Banner Mini-Guide series, we'll look at how the Psalms help us worship, pray, learn, counsel, and witness. We'll also explore what the Psalms teach us about blessing and cursing. Yes, there are Psalms that teach us how to curse! If you struggle with painful emotions, be encouraged, because we'll look at how to get free therapy via the Psalms.

And if you're convinced about the value of the Psalms but wonder how to actually add them to your life, family, or church services, I'll give you some practical tips on how to integrate the Psalms into these areas towards the end of the book. Everything is then rounded off with a five-step plan for interpreting the Psalms and some suggestions for further reading.

Imagine how happy Jesus will be to hear the songs he co-wrote, sang, and released, being sung again by those for whom he wrote them. Let's join Jesus in singing the songs of Jesus to Jesus!

1

Why the Psalms?

'The Psalms in the Christian Life? Is that not a contra-diction in terms? Aren't the Psalms just distant songs by distant people in the distant past from a distant place? Of what possible relevance or use are they to me today?'

'The Psalms are songs about ancient history; I live in the digital age.'

'The Psalms are rather depressing; I really need a mood boost.'

'The Psalms are complicated and hard to learn; I much prefer simple and catchy songs.'

'The Psalms are Old Testament worship; I live in the New Covenant age.'

'The Psalms don't mention Jesus; I want to sing about his wonderful name. So, why should the Psalms have any place in the Christian life?'

God's command
First, because God commands it. Twice the apostle Paul instructs us to sing psalms, hymns, and spiritual songs

(Eph. 5:19; Col. 3:16). Some people argue that these three categories of song are all found in the book of Psalms, meaning Paul is actually making the case for singing the Psalms only. Whether this is right or wrong, at the very least we can see that we have been commanded to sing the Psalms in the New Testament as well as in the Old (Psa. 105:2). Clearly this is not an optional extra or a matter of personal preference.

Christ's example

Second, we have the model of Christ and the apostles. Of course, there are many examples of God's people using the Psalms in the Old Testament, but there are also examples in the New. As we will see, the Lord and his apostles quote from the book of Psalms more often than any other Old Testament book. Jesus and his apostles sang from the Psalms together on the eve of his crucifixion (Matt. 26:30).[1] Jesus took the words of the Psalms upon his lips many times, even as he was dying (Psa. 22:1; Matt. 27:46), and the apostles used the Psalms to interpret New Testament events (Psa. 16:8-11; Acts 2:25-28).

Church tradition

Although our modern age tends to look down on the past and think that everything new is good and everything old is bad, the Bible encourages us to carefully consider and learn from the past (Deut. 4:9; Rom. 15:4; 2 Thess. 3:6).

---

[1] It was traditional to sing Psalms 113–118 (the 'Hallel Psalms') to accompany the Passover.

Although we should never do anything just because 'it has always been done this way,' if something has always been done, it is worth considering seriously, especially if it matches the Bible's commands and examples. Church history tells us that the Psalms have played a central role in the life of the church throughout the ages, and that it is only in the last one hundred and fifty years or so that they have begun to reduce in the church's life, even to the point of being forgotten in some cases.

Christian communion

The Psalms are a way to unite not only with Christians from the past but with Christians from all over the world. While every nation and culture has their own unique hymns and choruses, the Psalms are a universal songbook. When we sing them, we know that innumerable Christians all over the world are singing the same songs to the same God. Even if we are in a small fellowship of Christians, by singing the Psalms we join in communion with the worldwide church, singing the same songs to the same Saviour.

Divine inspiration

While many spiritual songs are inspiring, only the Psalms are inspired by God. God has provided us with a hymn-book that he has written and approved. We can therefore be sure that when we are singing the Psalms, we are singing what pleases God and is accepted by him. As they are divinely inspired, we can be confident that we are singing the truth about God, about ourselves, about our world, and about salvation.

5

God-centred world-view

While some worship songs can be overly subjective and too centred on the human singer, the Psalms offer a healthy corrective to this. As we will see in a later chapter, while the Psalms certainly deal with personal feelings and personal situations, they major on objective truth about God, revealing many facts about God in order to help individual believers with their personal situations and feelings. The Psalms, therefore, fundamentally re-orient the Christian's world-view, placing God at the centre and seeing everything in the light of God's character, words, and works. That changes the way we view the world and our place in it. We can see that humanity is so weak, so fragile, so transitory, and so sinful to the point that, when placed in contrast to God, we ask, 'What is man?' (Psa. 8:4; 144:3). The Psalms raise God so high that we look all the smaller in contrast.

Realistic variety

Various surveys have been conducted into the songs that are most sung in worship services, and they almost uniformly found that the vast majority focus on joy and confidence. While there are multiple psalms that express exuberant emotions such as praise (Psa. 8, 24, 29, 33, 47), thanksgiving (18, 66, 107, 118, 138), confidence (23, 121, 131), and happy memories (78, 105, 106, 136), there are also psalms of lament that express the pain of suffering, persecution, unbelief, anger, and injustice (*e.g.* 37, 39, 51, 86, 88, 120). There are psalms that call for blessing and psalms that call for cursing (35, 69, 109). There are psalms that express great confidence in God's reward of the righteous and punishment of the wicked (1, 127), and psalms that protest against the mystery of God's providence (73). This diversity and variety is a much more accurate depiction of the everyday Christian life. Reflecting these themes in private and public worship helps the Christian to be more real, more authentic, more transparent, and more honest in his or her worship. The Psalms tell us to stop pretending and to get real.

Wisely arranged

While some churches do try to incorporate the Psalms into the worship and sermons, it tends to be a bit of a 'Pick 'n Mix' approach, involving the three or four better known psalms such as Psalm 23 or Psalm 100. However, this is to miss the beautiful relationship between the Psalms and the way the Hebrew editors collected and arranged them.

For example, think about why Psalm 1 was placed first and Psalm 150 was placed last. Is there a reason that Psalm 1 calls us to study the message of the Psalms closely and then Psalm 2 presents the message of the divine King? Look at the sequence of Psalms 21–24 and ask why they go in that order. Also consider why Psalms 113–118 were sung on the evening of the Passover; or why Psalms 120–134 were sung as pilgrims journeyed to Jerusalem for the annual feasts. Look out for other fascinating connections between the Psalms, especially for any relationships between the psalms before and after the one you are reading or singing.

Another significant arrangement that is found in the Hebrew text of the Psalms is the division of the Psalter into five books.

Book 1.	Psalms 1–41
Book 2.	Psalms 42–72
Book 3.	Psalms 73–89
Book 4.	Psalms 90–106
Book 5.	Psalms 107–150

Each of these books concludes with a doxology, the fifth concluding with a series of doxologies. Some have argued that these five volumes have an overall narrative that traces the rise and fall of the Davidic monarchy, moving from promise and hope (Books 1 and 2), through disaster (Book 3), to renewed promise and hope (Books 4 and 5). These organizational features call for careful attention to the message in their arrangement.

Memorable truth

One of the great advantages of poetry is that it makes a deeper impression on the mind and heart and therefore is easier to memorize. Hebrew poetry is no different. Although it doesn't use rhyme, it does use metre, imagery, and repetition to make the truth stick better to our Teflon-like minds. Admittedly, some of the power of Hebrew poetry is lost in translation into English in our Bibles. That's why it may be better to use an English psalter, which will at least aim to involve metre and perhaps also rhyme. Singing such psalms presses the truth of God deep into our minds and hearts. How many Christians have recalled the psalms they learned as children in later seasons of trial or triumph! So important was memorizing the psalter to the ancient church that the Second Council of Nicaea decided that bishops must have memorized the entire psalter!

Maturing faith

Some psalms are deep, dense, and demanding. Others are difficult to understand, especially when we initially encounter them. In contrast with many modern songs, they often require considerable effort to figure out what they mean and how they apply to our lives. However, they reward careful and consistent study. One of the best pieces of advice I was given as a young Christian was to read a few verses of the Psalms every day. I've done that now for almost thirty years, and while I must admit there are still psalms that challenge my limited mind, the constant exposure to the Psalms has gradually grown my understanding and appreciation. One theologian has noted how the sixteenth-century French reformer John Calvin grew in his love for and use of the psalter. For example, in the first edition of his book *The Institutes of the Christian Religion* the Psalter is the least-quoted biblical book, but in the last edition he quotes it more than any other with the one exception of the epistle to the Romans.[1] The book of Psalms not only matures our faith but reflects mature faith.

---

[1] Herman J. Selderhuis, *Calvin's Theology of the Psalms* (Grand Rapids: Baker Academic, 2007), p. 16.

Sanctifying power

God uses his word to sanctify us (Eph. 5:26). Therefore, the more contact with God's truth we can experience, the more opportunity there is to grow in holiness. As songs stay with us longer than ordinary spoken or written words, the songs we sing will have a powerful impact on our spirituality. That's why the apostle calls us to have the word of Christ living richly in our hearts by singing psalms, hymns, and spiritual songs (Col. 3:16).

Christ revealed

Perhaps the greatest reason of all to incorporate the Psalms into our Christian lives is that they are so 'Christian': they are so full of Christ. That is why we will devote the whole of the next chapter to this subject. One of the reasons that people may have for ignoring the Psalms is that they belong to the pre-Christian era and therefore to pre-Christian worship. If I can show you how Christ-centred the Psalms are, I believe you will then have much greater motivation not only to continue reading this book, but to read, study, and sing the Psalms.

2

Christ in the Psalms[1]

C hrist in the Psalms? How can Christ be in the Psalms when they were written many hundreds of years before he came to earth? The simplest way to answer that question is to point to what Jesus and his apostles said of the Psalms. On the road to Emmaus, Jesus rebuked two of his disciples for their ignorance and unbelief. He said that if they had really known and believed what was written of him in the Old Testament, they would have understood the crucifixion and expected his resurrection (Luke 24:25-27). A few verses later, he instructs the rest of his disciples similarly, making explicit mention of the prophecies in the book of Psalms about him (Luke 24:44). The apostles also appeal explicitly to the Psalms as prophetic support for the person and work of Christ (*e.g.* Acts 2:25-28; 4:25, 26; 13:33).

So, with that warrant from Christ and his apostles in hand, I want to show you three ways we can use the Psalms to praise Christ.

[1] Adapted from David Murray, 'Christ's Poets,' in *Jesus on Every Page* (Nashville: Thomas Nelson, 2013).

We sing to Jesus with the Psalms

Most of the Psalms address God in general. But, as God is three persons, when we sing to God we are worshipping all three persons of the Godhead even though we are not saying their individual names. Therefore, when we sing of God as our Shield (Psa. 28:7), our Rock (18:2), our Shepherd (23:1), our Judge (7:11), our Refuge (46:1), our Fortress (31:3), our Creator (8:1, 6), our Healer (30:2), our Provider (78:23-29), and so on, we are singing to the Son of God as well as to the Father and the Holy Spirit, who are all equal in power and glory.

In the last chapter, we mentioned the different kinds of psalms we find in the Bible, all of which can be used in a Christ-centred way. For example, we can use the psalms of lament to confess our sins to Jesus. We can sing the psalms of praise to celebrate Jesus' person and work. We can sing the psalms of remembrance to look back on Jesus' acts throughout redemptive history. We can sing the psalms of confidence to express our faith in Jesus' salvation. We can sing the wisdom psalms to acknowledge that Jesus is our only source and perfect model of wisdom. We sing the psalms of thanksgiving to express our gratitude for Jesus' daily grace in our times of need. I encourage you to think of Jesus specifically when the Psalms mention 'God,' 'Lord,' or 'Jehovah.' In that way we sing *to* Jesus with the Psalms.

We sing of Jesus in the Psalms

I want to now move on to psalms that speak more specifically of Christ in a prophetic way, sometimes called the

'Messianic Psalms' as they speak of the coming Messiah (God's Anointed Saviour). How many of these are there?

Consider these statistics:

• The New Testament quotes from the psalter more often than from any other Old Testament book.

• Of the 283 direct quotes of the Old Testament in the New, 116 (41%) are from the Psalms.

• The Psalms are used more than fifty times in the Gospels to allude to the person and work of Jesus Christ.

• When the author of Hebrews sought biblical proof that Jesus was God, at least seven of his citations were from the book of Psalms.[1]

Although experts argue about some of these figures, at the very minimum, the New Testament identifies fifteen psalms that explicitly predict Christ's person and work. They include predictions such as Psalm 2 and Psalm 110, which refer to persons and events that have no human precedent or equivalent. They transcend anything any historical king has ever experienced.

However, it is not necessary for the New Testament to specifically identify a reference to Christ for a psalm to be regarded as Messianic. It is likely that these New Testament references are simply samples of how Christ is predicted in the Psalms. Since most of these references focus on Christ as the ultimate King of Israel, it would appear that God designed the office of king in general, and King David's life in particular, to be predictive of this future King. God

[1] Murray, *Jesus on Every Page*, p. 189.

ordained people, events, and institutions to be predictive pictures of the person and work of Christ. To put it another way, God works throughout history in patterns that anticipate future events.

This encourages us to think of Christ wherever we see references to the king or David in the Psalms. When we read the Psalms, we are reading of a real king, with a real kingdom, facing real enemies, and winning real victories. However, these are but predictive pictures of a similar but greater King, kingdom, enemies, and victory. This means that while there was an original human author intentionally writing of events present to him, there was also a divine author working alongside and through the human author to write of future events. David wrote psalms about his own kingship, but in terms that described a much larger throne, King, and kingdom to come.

You might be asking, 'But did David and the other psalmists grasp that they were predicting Christ and his salvation?' Having seen the fulfilment, we have the benefit of hindsight to identify these connections. But how much foresight did they have? Although they didn't know as much as those who live on the other side of the incarnation of Christ, they knew enough to know that they were not just writing about themselves and their times. For example, the apostle Peter says that David knew he was predicting the resurrection of Christ when he composed Psalm 16 (Acts 2:31). Peter also tells us in his first epistle that the Old Testament prophets, which included David, knew that they were predicting the sufferings and glory of

Christ that would bring salvation to the world, although they also knew that future generations would see this even more clearly than they did (1 Pet. 1:10-13).

Putting all the different kinds of predictions together, we can construct a Christology from the Psalms, a system of truths that tells us so much about the future Messianic King. Look especially for these truths as you study and sing the Psalms, and you will find they turn into Christ-centred songs of praise:

- Sin has messed up the world and humanity desperately needs a royal deliverer.
- God will graciously send a royal deliverer.
- The royal deliverer will reveal God in an unprecedented way.
- The royal deliverer will suffer as a sacrifice for sin.
- The royal deliverer will reign as God's King everywhere and forever.

And if you want more specifics, then consider the following more detailed connections:

Psalm	Prediction	Fulfilment
2:7	The King will be the Son of God	Matt. 3:17; Acts 13:33
8:2	The King will be praised by children	Matt. 21:15, 16
8:3-5	The King will be the Son of man	Heb. 2:5-9
8:6	The King will rule over everything	Heb. 2:8

15

Psalm	Prediction	Fulfilment
16:10	The King will rise from the dead	Matt. 28:7
22:1	The King will be forsaken by God	Matt. 27:46
22:7, 8	The King will be mocked by his enemies	Luke 23:35
22:16	The King's hands and feet will be pierced	John 20:27
22:18	The King's clothes will be gambled for	Matt. 27:35, 36
34:20	The King's bones will not be broken	John 19:32, 33, 36
35:11	The King will be accused by false witnesses	Mark 14:57
41:9	The King will be betrayed by a friend	Luke 22:47
45:6	The King will reign forever	Heb. 1:8
68:18	The King will ascend to heaven	Acts 1:9-11
69:9	The King will zealously reform God's house	John 2:17
69:21	The King will be given vinegar and gall	Matt. 27:34
109:8	The King will replace his betrayer	Acts 1:20
110:1	The King will rule over his enemies	Matt. 22:44

Psalm	Prediction	Fulfilment
110:4	The King will be an eternal priest	Heb. 5:6
118:22	The King will be the chief cornerstone	Matt. 21:42
118:26	The King will come in the name of the Lord	Matt. 21:9

We sing with Jesus in the Psalms

We not only sing *to* and *of* Jesus in the Psalms, we also sing *with* him. How so? Well, the Psalms were Jesus' hymnbook throughout his earthly life. When we sing the Psalms, we are singing the songs Jesus sang. How amazing is that! If they were good enough for him, they are good enough for me!

Think of how older Christians often fall back on songs they learned in Sunday School to help them through tough times. Spiritual songs appropriate to their spiritual condition come naturally to their memories. There are examples in the New Testament of this also being Jesus' experience (*e.g.* Psa. 22:1 and Matt. 27:46; Psa. 31:5 and Luke 23:46; Psa. 110:1 and Matt. 22:44). But this was likely the common and constant experience in his soul. The Psalms, therefore, give us an accurate and intimate insight into the soul of Jesus. The Gospels focus largely on his outward public life; but the Psalms give us his secret inner life.

When people write biographies, they often try to guess the thoughts of the subject, but here we do not need to guess. God so ordered the psalmists' lives, and so inspired their reflections, that they anticipated Jesus' thoughts and feelings. Jesus found himself and his experiences in the psalmists and their experiences and therefore used their songs at appropriate moments in his life.

We may worship Jesus in the Psalms by meditating on when and how he sang them. As you sing the psalms of praise, think of how Jesus used the same psalms to praise his heavenly Father (Psa. 8, 24, 29, 33, 47, 48). Think of how mournfully he sang the psalms of lament as he saw the impact of sin on himself, the church, and the community (38, 51, 86, 120); how anxiously he sang the psalms of suffering as he anticipated the sacrificial pains that lay ahead for him (22, 69); how joyfully he sang the psalms of thanksgiving for the many deliverances he experienced (18, 66, 107, 118, 138); how boldly he sang the psalms of confidence as he entrusted himself to his heavenly Father (121, 131); how gladly he sang the psalms of remembrance as he recalled God's great acts in the past (78, 105, 106, 136); how powerfully he sang the royal psalms especially as he looked forward to his post-cross exaltation and worldwide reign (2, 20, 21, 24, 45, 47, 72, 110); how holily he sang the imprecatory psalms when he saw the spiritual devastation his enemies were causing (58–59, 109).

Just as certain psalms seem to especially fit certain seasons of our lives, so the Psalms fitted the many stages of Jesus' life. Look up the following Psalm references as you think of how Jesus would have understood and used the Psalms when he was a young boy (Psa. 8:2), when he was a teenager (119:9), when he went to the synagogue (5:7), when he was carrying out his morning devotions (5:3), when he read the Scriptures (12:6), when he reflected on his preaching (40:9), when he defeated temptation (91:7), when he woke (3:5), when he slept (4:8), when he watched the devil at work (10:8, 9), when he saw souls saved (3:8), when he heard of the deaths of his followers (12:1), when he celebrated the Passover with his unique and unparalleled understanding (118:17-29), when the cross loomed (55:4, 5), in the Garden of Gethsemane (116:13), when falsely accused (2:1, 2), when betrayed (55:12-14), when he died (31:5), when he rose again (16), when he anticipated the judgment of the wicked (11:6), when he ascended (68).

What insight the book of Psalms gives us into Jesus' spiritual life! What a privilege that we can sing Jesus' hymns from his own hymn-book! As his body, we can sing the Psalms not only to Jesus or of Jesus, but *with* Jesus, our Head. He is our Worship Leader.

3

Worshipping in the Psalms

One theologian said a Christian should be 'a Hallelujah from head to foot.' I can't say I've always agreed with this. When I was a young Christian, worship just happened before what I thought was the main event—the sermon. Singing was like soup or salad; you had to eat it to get to the steak. Now, thirty years later, worship is often my favourite Christian experience. I'm not a great singer, but I do love to sing God's praises with God's people in God's house.

While this book will highlight many uses of the Psalms, their primary use is as songs of praise. The Psalms are to be sung to God as worship. The word 'psalms' comes from the Greek version of the Old Testament, which entitled the book *psalmoi*. This is related to a word meaning 'pluck a stringed instrument,' and was often used simply to describe a song. The original Hebrew title, *sepher tehillim*, also means 'book of praises.' Many of the individual titles of the Psalms make clear they were intended for public worship. So, whatever we do with the Psalms, we must sing them and sing them as songs of worship to God. Let's therefore look at what this book of worship songs teaches us about worship.

The imperative of worship

The first lesson is that worshipping God is not an option. It is repeatedly commanded throughout the Psalms (Psa. 9:11; 22:23; 33:2; 47:6, 7; 66:2, 8; 100:4). It is really the positive side of the first two commandments (Exod. 20:1-6). The first forbids worshipping any other God apart from the true God, and the second forbids worshipping God with any man-made worship. But there is a positive side that is also implied in these commands. If that is what God forbids, then it must also reveal what he requires: that he alone is to be worshipped and he is to be worshipped in the way he prescribes. That's what comes out again and again in the Psalms. They command us to worship God using these songs that God has provided. Before sin came into the world, worship was as natural as breathing. It hardly needed to be commanded. But since sin has entered and upset everything, the act of worship is now commanded and the way of worship is prescribed, and disobedience will be punished. I hope you feel the weight of the divine imperative throughout the Psalms as we are reminded again and again to praise God.

The reason for worship

Although he could have, God chose not to simply issue bare commands to worship. He might have said, 'Praise me,' and if we asked why, he could have replied, 'Because

I said so.' Instead, he provided multiple reasons to praise him. He argues us into worship, as it were. He addresses our minds with information about himself with a view to moving our hearts and wills to praise him. Worship is therefore to be reasonable and rational (Psa. 47:7). Yes, human emotion must come into it, but only as a result of following divine logic. Any worship that is not reasonable is not worship. Mindless worship is godless worship. Thoughtful worship that leads to appropriate emotion is worship that gives maximum pleasure to God. Among the arguments that God presents to us in the Psalms are that he is to be worshipped for who he is, for what he has spoken, and for what he has done and is doing for his people (63:3; 103:1; 48:1; 103:2; 18:1, 2; 98:1, 2). Who cannot be persuaded that such a God is worthy of our worship (18:3)?

The place of worship

Many today claim that they can worship God anywhere and everywhere. That's true, but it's not the whole truth. Also, that truth must not be used, as it often is, to defend absence from public worship in the local church. By all means, worship God everywhere, but the Psalms insist that the foundation for worship is the public worship services in God's church with God's people (Psa. 5:7; 22:22, 25; 132:7). It doesn't end there, but it does begin there. If it doesn't begin there, it will end everywhere. Because, from what I've seen, those who choose not to worship in church eventually worship nowhere. The Psalms remind us that we need corporate worship: we need to regularly join with God's people in acts of public worship if we are going to continue as worshippers of God. God appears to put a special blessing and give his special presence to public gatherings of his people to worship him. Without that regular injection of public worship, we will not be inoculated against the godless spirit of the age and will soon be carried away with the virus of worldliness. Having said all that, if worship ends at church, then church-going will soon end too. While the psalmists clearly love worshipping with God's people, they continue to worship daily in their family lives and private lives (72:15). When do they do this? In one place a psalmist says he worships morning, noon, and evening (55:17), another worships seven times a day (119:64), and another all the day (71:8). Whatever the exact details, it's clear that they worship everywhere every day, but that is based upon worshipping with God's people in God's house.

The life of worship

I want to expand a little upon the idea of the whole of life as worship. While God is the object of worship and God's words and works are the primary content of worship, the psalmists bring their whole lives to God in worship. By that I mean they live their whole life before God in a worshipful spirit. They have no hesitation in bringing the ordinary stuff of life into worship. Indeed, they seem to make use of every little thing or incident in life, to turn it into worship. Our bedtime and rising time (Psa. 3:5; 4:7), insomnia (63:6), the lives of animals, birds, and fish (104), leaving the house and returning again (121:8), a long day's work (104:23), sailing

(107:23-32), babies in the womb (109:13-16), the challenges of youth (119:9), the beauty of marriage (45), raising children (128), finances (49), growing old (92:12-15), dying (6; 23), the stars and planets (8:3; 19:1-6), planting and harvesting (65:12, 13), changing seasons (147:15-18). We could go on and on. I would challenge you to find any life situation that is not found in the Psalms and turned into a matter of praise to God. And then I would challenge you to do the same in your own life so that you praise him more and more (71:14).

The spirit of worship

God wants us to worship him not only in truth but in the spirit (John 4:24). That means we not only have to be careful about what we use to worship God but how we worship him. We can have the most perfect songs and the most perfect music but have no real worship. So, what is it to worship God in the spirit?

It is to recognize our need of the Holy Spirit to animate our spirits. The psalmists prayed to God to enliven and revive them in worship (Psa. 80:18; 119:25). They knew that they couldn't do this on their own, that they needed the help of God's Spirit to truly worship God.

When God's Spirit is in us and with us, we will be resolved in our worship (Psa. 42:5, 11; 56:12; 57:7). We will be determined and purposeful not only to worship but to fix our hearts and minds on God as we worship (79:13). We will want to worship with our whole hearts, not just a part of them (9:1; 86:12), and we will stir up our whole souls to worship God (103:1). We are not going to just passively drift into worship. No, there must be active and vigorous intent. Why would we be less determined to worship God than we are to pass an exam, climb a mountain, beat our track time, and so on?

Spiritual worship is humble worship. Worship at its core is a glad willingness to recognize God's awesome greatness and our smallness. It's more than that, but it's at least that. It involves taking as low a place as possible before God and lifting up God as high as possible. It is the spirit of John the Baptist, 'He must increase and I must decrease.' That's why, throughout the Psalms, we find the psalmists bowing, prostrating themselves before God. This is a glad and willing reverence based on being a creature before our Creator, and even more on being a sinner before our Saviour. One of the ways to increase our pleasure in worship is to increase our reverence for God (89:7; 96:9).

Spiritual worship is loud worship. Yes, yes, I know it's possible to have massed choirs singing beautiful songs in a beautiful way and for there to be no worship. And yes, I know God looks on the heart, and that making melody in our hearts is the place that worship starts (1 Sam. 16:7; Eph. 5:19). But too often, these facts are used to excuse pathetic, lethargic, and mumbling worship. Is it not the case that what's in the heart must come out of the mouth (Matt. 15:18)? If it's in our hearts, it cannot but come out of our mouths eventually. When the psalmist tried to suppress his praises, he almost burst, and eventually had to let it out (Psa. 39:3). God is great and therefore greatly to be praised (48:1; 96:4), not just with our hearts but with our mouths (51:15; 98:4). We are to make a joyful noise to the Lord (98:4). Isn't it sad that people can sing secular songs, sporting songs, national songs, and country songs with greater fervour than the Lord's songs?

Spiritual worship is new worship. The psalmist said that God put a new song in his mouth (Psa. 40:3) and we are commanded to sing a new song to the Lord (96:1). This does not necessarily mean that we need to keep writing new songs. No, singing a new song can also mean singing old songs with new understanding, new sincerity, new depth, and new appreciation. That's a wonderful way to freshen up our worship.

The obedience of worship

One of the strange elements of the Psalms is how they contain ethical instructions. At first it seems a bit weird that songs of praise to God should contain directions for our daily lives (*e.g.* Psa. 15; 34:12-14; 101). However, it all makes sense when we realize that God hates hypocrisy. He hates people who praise him with their lips but their lives are offensive to him. He prefers obedience to sacrifice. We are to worship him in the beauty of holiness. That's why we can find supporting references for every one of the Ten Commandments in the psalter as well as contrasts with the lifestyles of the wicked.

The benefits of worship

The 'forgotten beatitude' reminds us that it is more blessed to give than to receive. But that's not just true of money. It's also true of praise. Although we may think getting praised is better for us, giving of praise, especially to God, is far more beneficial, far more blessed. God has designed worship of him not only to give glory to him but good to us. Let's give God the praise and honour he deserves and discover that it is indeed more blessed to give than to receive.

The end of worship

Sometimes worship is so good, we wish it could go on forever (Psa. 104:33). The wonderful news is that it will. Worship here is tuning our voices for heaven's eternal choir (52:9; 61:8). Whatever pleasure we have found in worship on earth, it is but a tiny sample of what we will enjoy forever in heaven. There, we will not only be top-to-toe hallelujahs but forever hallelujahs and perfect hallelujahs.

4

Praying the Psalms

How do I know what to pray for? How do I know if I am praying God's will or my will? How can I pray when I feel so dead and lifeless? How can I change my prayers from jumbled moans and groans into coherent petitions? How can I express my exuberant rejoicing in ways that honour God? How can I say what I really think to God?

The Psalms help us to answer all these questions by modelling what to pray for, by revealing God's will to us, by provoking and stimulating living prayer from dead hearts, by providing articulated expressions with which to clothe our groans, by enabling the safe expression of jubilant joy, and by authorizing us to say what we really think to God. The Psalms are not only God's approved hymn-book, but his approved prayer-book. Of all the books in the Bible, this one has the most to teach us about prayer and about how to pray. I want to begin by drawing some general lessons about prayer from the Psalms before turning to how to use the Psalms in prayer.

A book about prayer

Prayer is intimate

When we read the Psalms, we are permitted to eaves-drop on the most private and confidential area of human life—how people pray to God. We are allowed to listen in as individuals pour out their deepest concerns and express their innermost thoughts. As we do so, we think of removing our shoes because the ground feels so holy. What is usually so secret and sensitive is exposed for all to see and hear, and what we see and hear is an incredibly close relationship that could not be more transparent and trusting. False formality is banished, thoughts of impressing others are expelled, hypocrisy and pretence vanishes. It's just so real, gritty, and authentic. We are observing the beauty of trusting love and loving trust between two parties who have grown deeper and deeper in familiarity without ever lapsing into over-familiarity. What a challenge to emulate such sincerity and intimacy as we cultivate our own relationship to God in prayer.

Prayer starts with God

Just as in the Lord's Prayer, the psalmist usually begins with God's character, name, kingdom, and will. It's not a mere shopping list of self-centred daily demands; rather, he starts with God, and with that God-centred perspective he then begins to pray about his own life and situation. And having done that, he often returns to who God is and what God is doing.

Prayer is concrete

Having said all that, the psalmist gets to the point. No, he doesn't just charge up to God and demand. But neither does he go round and round in circles, multiplying vague and general words without ever getting specific and particular. Rather, after appropriate time for worship, praise, confession, and thanksgiving, he gets down to the business of life and beseeches God for help with the down-to-earth realities of his life.

Prayer is transformative

Although many of the Psalms begin in a mood of despair and doubt, they almost all end on a note of hope and confidence. The psalmist works through his issues in the light of God and finds that his dark mood slowly lifts, the sun breaks through, and he is lifted above himself. Prayer does not change God, and it may not change our situation, but it certainly changes us very much for the better.

Prayer is militant

The Psalms have an indubitable militancy about them. Their emphasis on spiritual warfare reminds us that 'we do not wrestle against flesh and blood, but against the rulers, against the authorities, against the cosmic powers over this present darkness, against the spiritual forces of evil in the heavenly places.' (Eph. 6:12). This is not a soft, cowardly, cautious religion, but a bold, brave, and combative one. We can almost smell the gunpowder, hear the rockets, and sense the ground shaking under us as the psalmists engage the enemy and call on God to appear for his people and act decisively for them in the face of terrible odds stacked against them. They remind us that 'the weapons of our warfare are not of the flesh but have divine power to destroy strongholds. We destroy arguments and every lofty opinion raised against the knowledge of God, and take every thought captive to obey Christ,' (2 Cor. 10:4, 5). What a wake-up call to a sleepy, fearful, and defensive church.

A book of prayers
Having identified some of the lessons about prayer in the Psalms, let us now examine how to use the Psalms as a prayer-book.

Direct prayers
Sometimes the Psalms just match our needs so perfectly that we don't need to change or adapt them to our situation. We just take them upon our lips and make the psalmist's words our words. This is part of the genius of the Psalms, that they have been so inspired by God that they fit so many different people in so many different ages, in so many different places, in so many different circumstances.

For example, the well-known and successful British politician Jonathan Aitken one day found himself in prison after being convicted of libel. He was from a wealthy, high-class English family and here he was in Belmarsh, one of the most notorious prisons in England. In his biography he relates how he felt on his first night in the cells when he started hearing the obscene taunts and threats of the other prisoners as they boasted to one another of what they would do to him. Aitken recounted:

> So I knelt down on the concrete floor and tried to say a prayer. Because I was so petrified by the shouts of menace around me, at first I found it impossible to say even the simplest words of supplication. Then I remembered that just before going off to the Old Bailey to be sentenced a friend had put in my pocket a calendar style booklet entitled *Praying the Psalms*. When I was searched on arrival at Belmarsh it was confiscated for drug examination by sniffer dogs. But it was later returned to me [...]. So I turned up the page for 8 June. It recommended reading Psalm 130. I studied its eight short verses which began: 'Out of the depths I cry to you, O Lord. Lord, hear my voice. Let your ears be attentive to my cry for mercy.' A warm and comforting wave of reassurance flooded over me. Suddenly I realized that I was not as lonely, scared, helpless or vulnerable as I had thought. The author of the Psalm had been there before me. Some 3,000 years earlier he had experienced very similar emotions of despair to mine. He had found a route to climb out of his depths with God's help and he had signposted that route in beautiful poetry recorded for posterity in the book of the Bible known as 'The Psalms.'[1]

As you get to know the Psalms, and especially as you memorize them, you will be amazed at how often they just

---

[1] Derek W. H. Thomas, 'Psalm Singing and Pastoral Theology,' in *Sing a New Song: Recovering Psalm Singing for the Twenty-First Century*, eds. Joel R. Beeke and Anthony T. Selvaggio (Grand Rapids: Reformation Heritage Books, 2010), pp. 166-7.

fit your need so perfectly and provide words so suitable for prayer.

Translated prayers

Other times, you will think that there does not seem to be much in the way of prayer language or prayer ideas in the psalms you are reading or singing. That's what I want to focus on now to help you to turn or 'translate' what seem like prayerless words into prayer-filled words. Let's take Psalm 46, one of the better-known psalms, as an example to work through. At appropriate points I'll 'translate' the psalm into prayers (highlighted in bold).

> ¹ *God is our refuge and strength,*
> *a very present help in trouble.*

O Lord, please be my refuge and strength when I am feeling scared and weak. Help me because I am in deep and present danger.

> ² *Therefore we will not fear*
> *though the earth gives way,*
> *though the mountains be moved into the heart of the sea;*
> ³ *though its waters roar and foam,*
> *though the mountains tremble at its swelling. Selah*

My Father, everything about me seems to be shaking. People and institutions, churches and governments, all of them seem so unstable and unreliable. I'm feeling anxious about the uncertainty and instability of the times and pray that you would take away fear, even if things go from bad

to worse. Remind me of who you are so that I can be quiet and calm even in the midst of deafening noise.

> ⁴ *There is a river whose streams make glad the city of God,*
>   *the holy habitation of the Most High.*

Above all, O God, remember your church, your city. May your house be a place where I and many others find joy no matter what else is going on in the world and in our little worlds. May the refreshing streams of your Holy Spirit satiate and satisfy your people.

> ⁵ *God is in the midst of her; she shall not be moved;*
>   *God will help her, when morning dawns.*

I am surrounded by enemies, my heavenly Captain. The night is dark and it looks like the walls are about to be breached. Ride to our rescue, Lord of the heavenly armies. Come to our help, Helper of the helpless. Even at the last moment, come and stabilize and secure your church. Whatever else is going on outside, be in our midst, be at the centre of our worship and of our lives.

> ⁶ *The nations raged, the kingdoms totter;*
>   *he utters his voice, the earth melts.*

Speak, O Lord. Speak against the raging nations on earth and the angry powers of hell. Speak in such a way that shows your voice is far more powerful than the accumulated anger of my enemies. Speak in the preaching of the gospel and speak in demonstrations of your providence.

⁷ *The Lord of hosts is with us;*
  The God of Jacob is our fortress.   Selah

I totally trust you, my Lord and God. Just as you looked after undeserving Jacob, I believe you will look after me. I want to pause and remember how your past dealings with your people assure me of your unchanging faithfulness.

⁸ *Come, behold the works of the Lord,*
  how has brought desolations on the earth.
⁹ *He makes wars cease to the end of the earth;*
  he breaks the bow and shatters the spear;
  he burns the chariots in the fire.

I praise you, Lord, for what you have done and are doing without any help from me. I praise you for every single work of yours that I see in the earth: your works of creation, providence, and redemption. I praise you for ending wars and trace all peace in the world to you. I continue to pray for war-torn areas of the world, that you would bring about peace. I pray that you would bless those who are waging just war, that you would bless them with safety and speedy victory. I pray for your church and your people to emerge victorious against every enemy.

¹⁰ *Be still, and know that I am God.*

Yes, God, I am stilling my soul and seeking stillness in my life in order that I can know you are God. I know that if I have no stillness or silence in my life that I cannot know you. Therefore help me to be still and know that you are God. Help me to make time for stillness in my

daily, weekly, and annual schedule so that I can grow in my knowledge of you.

> *I will be exalted among the nations,*
> *I will be exalted in the earth!*

Keep your promise, Lord. Be lifted up, not only in my life but throughout all the earth. May Jesus be raised higher and higher in people's minds, hearts, mouths, and actions. May his kingdom come and his will be done on earth as in heaven.

> [11] *The Lord of hosts is with us;*
> *The God of Jacob is our fortress. Selah*

I leave this prayer reminding myself that you are with me, that you will never leave me or forsake me. Help me therefore to go and make disciples with this confidence. And I do so humbled by the remembrance that I'm no better than Jacob, but just as you were his refuge in the midst of his sins and trials, so you will be with me.

I hope you can see how easy it is to turn an ancient prayer into a present plea. How to take God's hymn-book and turn it into God's prayer-book.

5

Learning from the Psalms

Although many modern cultures teach and learn using logic, systematic analysis, and so on, older cultures, especially Middle Eastern cultures, often taught using songs. There's a reason for that, of course—songs stick. They are easier to learn and stay with us longer than ordinary didactic teaching. That was especially important in a culture that did not have much in the way of written materials to teach with, and very few people could read anyway. The solution to that was stories and songs. God taught Old Testament Israel using narratives and poetry set to music. Therefore, when we come to the Psalms, we are coming not just to have a sing-song that will make us all feel better, but to learn theology.

In fact, at the risk of destroying the poetic genre in which this theology was delivered, we can extract and construct a systematic theology from the Psalms. Let me give you a sampling of this and think about how you can expand and add to this as you sing the Psalms. Remember, this is nowhere near exhaustive.

Doctrine of Scripture

Psalm 19 and Psalm 119 are the primary places to discover the Psalms' doctrine of Scripture. Why not read Psalm 119 and write down everything that psalm teaches you about the word of God? You'll need a few days! In the meantime, let me show you what Psalm 19 teaches about Holy Scripture.

After narrating how God speaks in the sky (Psa. 19:1-6), the psalmist shows how God speaks in the Scriptures (verses 7-9). As the sun is the way God shines light into the dark physical world, so the Scriptures are the way God shines light into the darkened spiritual world. These verses describe God's word and its effects in a bit more detail:

It revives the soul (verse 7a)

'Revive' can mean to refresh, convert or transform by returning to the original state. If you follow the Bible's instructions, it will transform your life, your whole life, your inner life. It is a comprehensive message for a comprehensive change. Its whole message can pull your whole life together. It can mould your soul into its proper shape so that you fit into God's role for you in his world.

It makes the simple wise (verse 7b)

'Testimony' means 'divine witness.' In the Bible we have God testifying who he is and what he requires. Unlike the untrustworthy witness of men, God's testimony is 'sure.' It is unwavering and immovable. It can be trusted. We can reliably build our lives upon it. The Hebrew word for 'simple' is the word used to describe an open door. In the

Psalms, 'simple' is used positively to describe someone who is open to God's word and is teachable. As such, he or she is skilled to apply the word of God in every area of life. She is able to make the right decisions about the right things at the right times. She knows when to open the door and when to shut it, what to let into her mind and what to keep out.

It makes the sad happy (verse 8a)

You may have been lost one day in the woods or in a strange city. You felt disoriented and worried. Then you saw a landmark, something you recognized. Your fear dissipated and joy filled your heart as you finally knew which way to go. So it is for the Christian in this world. She can be confused and uncertain as to the way ahead. She begins reading the Scriptures, and then comes across clear direction for her life. She can now go on her way rejoicing. She has a new sense of direction. The right path may not be the easy path but it is the joyful path.

It gives clarity to the confused (verse 8b)

'Commandment' emphasizes the authoritative prescriptions of Scripture. It is binding and not optional. The Bible does not come with suggestions or proposals but with commandments. These commands enlighten the eyes. The world is full of blind people living in darkness. They are full of questions. What is truth/error? What is right/wrong? What should I do? What is the meaning of life? What is the purpose of life? Into this dark confusion the word of God comes with bright clarity and says, 'This is the way, walk in it.'

It cleans the dirty forever (verse 9a)

'Fear of the Lord' is a synonym for Holy Scripture. It puts the effect (fear) for the cause (Scripture). The effect of reading Scripture should be fear and reverence of God. Unlike men's words, which are always tainted, God's word is holy and separate from sin. And it has a purifying effect. It teaches us to fear the Lord, which in turn causes us to depart from evil. The word of God was cleansing sinners thousands of years ago and its cleansing power continues to this day.

It pre-judges character and conduct (verse 9b)

'Rules' or 'judgments' are the divine verdicts issued from the bench of the Judge of all the earth. He is the supreme Judge of the Supreme Court. By reading his word, we can know his rulings or judgments before we go to his bench. The Bible has pre-released them so that, knowing what happens to those who die in sin and to those who die in Christ, we can take appropriate action.

Doctrine of God

It's especially in the area of doctrine about God that the Psalms differ from so many other theological tomes. You won't find long philosophical treatments here about the being and attributes of God. The language is much simpler but no less profound.

The Psalms celebrate God as Trinity: as Father (Psa. 68:5; 103:13), as Son (2:7; 110), and as Holy Spirit (51:11; 104:30; 136:33; 139:7; 143:10).

They celebrate God in his attributes: as eternal (Psa. 90:2), as patient (145:8), as faithful (89:1), as holy (99:9), as just (145:17), as good (145:9), as powerful (29), as wise (139), and so on.

They celebrate God in his works: as the Creator (8, 19, 104), as the Director of history (105, 106), as the Protector (91), as the Provider (50), as the Covenanter (89), as the King (93, 97), as the Judge (50, 94, 96), as the Forgiver (51, 130), and as the Shepherd (23).

Doctrine of humanity

The Psalmist worships God for creating holy humanity with royal dignity and dominion (Psa. 8). However, he grieves that humanity is now fallen, sinful, and sin-addicted (14:1-3). Sin has not only resulted in a frail humanity that is slowly dying (49:6-14) but a sinful humanity that is offensive to God (78:58, 59) and liable to divine punishment (90:1-11; 107:17, 18). Sin not only impacts the deepest parts of the human heart (51:5-11), and every part of human existence (40:12), but the furthest parts of the earth. Sin, therefore, is to be confessed (51:4, 5) and forsaken (34:14).

Having said all that about sin, how then do we explain the psalms in which the psalmist protests his innocence and integrity, often basing his prayers upon these protests? These are sometimes called psalms of vindication (*e.g.* Psa. 7:3-5; 15; 17:1-4; 26). How do we understand them? Obviously it cannot mean he thought he was sinless and righteous. Some explain this by saying that the psalmist had a 'relative righteousness.' He is not perfect, but relative to his enemies, compared with the wicked, he is much more innocent and righteous than they are. However, it is more likely that he is referring to specific false accusations. He is not describing his whole life but only the areas he is being falsely accused in.[1]

Doctrine of Christ

For the doctrine of Christ in the Psalms see chapter two, 'Christ in the Psalms.'

Doctrine of salvation

How is a person saved in the Psalms? Is there a doctrine of salvation in the Psalms, and is it the same as the New Testament doctrine of salvation? Were the psalmists saved by grace alone, by faith alone, in Christ alone, to the glory of God alone? I believe that they were and that the soteriology (the teaching about salvation) of the Psalms is the same as we find in John 3:16 and the rest of the New Testament. We can say this because Christ and the apostles so often used the language, concepts, and theology of the Psalms to explain Christ's person and work.

Also, ask yourself this question: who is the Redeemer in the Psalms? Is it the psalmist or God? The uniform message is that it is God alone that saves (Psa. 3:8; 40:1-5; 49:7-15; 103:10-12; 130). What does the psalmist do to be saved by God? Does he contribute anything? No. He calls upon God (50:15), he seeks the Lord (34:4), he looks to God (34:5), he

---

[1] See Richard P. Belcher Jr., *The Messiah and the Psalms: Preaching Christ from All the Psalms* (Ross-Shire: Christian Focus, 2014), pp. 89-93.

cries to God (34:6), he waits upon God (130:5), he depends on God alone (62:5). All of these are synonyms for faith. There's not a hint of human contribution here. All the stress is on divine activity.

Did the psalmists believe in Christ, though? Or was it just a general faith in God? Although they obviously never saw Christ as clearly as we do, they saw enough and believed enough to be saved by Christ (1 Pet. 1:10-12). Christ himself says that David knew his descendant would also be the divine Messiah (Matt. 22:45; Psa. 110:1), and remember the apostle Peter says that David knew he was prophesying about the Messiah's resurrection (Acts 2:30, 31). They all understood the need for a sacrifice to draw near to God (Psa. 50:5) and yet also understood that animal sacrifices were not enough (50:8-15). Psalm 118 anticipates that the stone which the builders will reject will be the chief cornerstone and that this will mark the coming of the Messiah in the name of the Lord (118:22-27).

And if you are still doubting, here's one last question: who gets the glory in the Psalms? All the psalmists unite in saying, 'Not to us, O Lord, not to us, but to your name give glory, for the sake of your steadfast love and your faithfulness!' (Psa. 115:1). The salvation is by grace alone, by faith alone, in Christ alone, to the glory of God alone.

Doctrine of the church

The Psalms were composed to be sung together in the covenant community of God's people. They assume that God's people will gather together to worship their God. Although the word 'covenant' only appears explicitly in twelve psalms, it is the major focus of both Psalms 89 and 132.[1] Also, God's covenant name of Jehovah (Yahweh) is used over six hundred times. This not only guards us against individualism but also reminds us that the church is a family, bound together with God's unbreakable covenant bonds. The church and its worship are to be marked by holiness, by great care and reverence in dealing with God and worship (Psa. 2:11; 96:9). But this is not some strict, ugly legalism; rather, this kind of holiness beautifies the church (29:2).

Doctrine of the last things

'Eschatology' means literally 'the last things,' and is a study of how human life ends and how the world ends. There is not as much detail in the Psalms about the last things as there is about many other theological topics. This is partly because Christ had not come yet and therefore it was not possible to teach or understand these things as clearly as New Testament Christians would. However, there is more teaching about this subject in the Psalms than is usually realized.

As we have already seen, the Psalms emphasize that human life will end with death. But they also go on to

[1] Raymond Dillard and Tremper Longman III, *Introduction to the Old Testament* (Grand Rapids: Zondervan, 1995), p. 228.

describe the afterlife. The Psalmist believes in a resurrection of the body that will lead to a joyful and pleasure-filled eternity (Psa. 16:9-11). He anticipates that one day he will wake up, open his eyes, and not only see the Lord but be like him (17:15). That's why the death of Christians is revealed as precious in God's sight (116:15). The final judgment is also a frequent topic to be sung about, partly to warn the wicked, but partly also to rejoice in God's judgment (2:4-6, 10-12; 11:6; 49:14, 15; 96–98).

Now, do you see how much theology is in the Psalms? No, it isn't taught in a structured and systematic way like this, but rather in a form that would stick. As these songs were sung, huge theological truths were being taught and learned, almost effortlessly. They may not have realized it, but the Israelite psalm-singers were brilliant theologians, and so can we be if we imbibe the Psalms and they become part and parcel of our being. This is not to say that every theological truth was fully revealed in the Psalms; it is to say that every theological truth is there at least in seed form in the Psalms. No wonder the German reformer Martin Luther called the psalter the 'little Bible,' for 'most beautifully and briefly it embraces everything in the entire Bible; it is made into a fine enchiridion, or handbook.'[1]

[1] Ewald M. Plass, *What Luther Says: A Practical In-Home Anthology for the Active Christian* (St. Louis: Concordia, 1959), p. 999.

6

Painting in the Psalms

In the previous chapter, we noted how one of the most effective ways to teach children was to use songs. Another is to use pictures, either pictorial images or word pictures. That's because pictures are not only easier to understand than words, but usually make a deeper and longer impression than words. We find this teaching strategy frequently in the Bible, especially in Hebrew poetry like the Psalms.

Typology

The Old Testament predicted Christ's person and work with prophetic words and prophetic pictures. These prophetic pictures are sometimes called 'types,' the study of them is called 'typology,' and the fulfilments are called 'antitypes' (*lit.* in place of the types). Typology basically means 'picture-ology,' which indicates a kind of visual theology where God gives a picture of the truth in order to preach the truth. A 'type' is a real person, place, object, or event that God ordained to act as a predictive pattern or resemblance of Christ's person and work, or of opposition to both. Let's unpack that a little:

- *A type is a real person, place, object or event*: it is true, real, and factual, not a made-up allegory.
- *That God ordained*: it does not resemble Christ's person or work by mere coincidence but by divine plan.
- *To act as a predictive pattern or resemblance*: the same truth is found in the Old Testament picture and the New Testament fulfilment.
- *Of Christ's person and work*: the truth in the picture is enlarged, heightened, and clarified in the fulfilment.
- *Or of opposition to both*: God also gave prophetic pictures of Christ's enemies.

The foundation of typology is that the same gospel truths are presented in both Testaments—though presented in different ways. That is why the Old Testament institutions are called shadows of gospel truths. Whilst a shadow is not as clear as what is casting the shadow, there is a likeness and resemblance with what casts the shadow. We are looking for the same truths in both the type and its fulfilment.

These types were ideally suited to the Old Testament church's Eastern mindset. We in the West are so used to oral and written teaching from an early age that it is hard for us to imagine how the Israelites could learn through other means as well. However, the Eastern mind with its more contemplative traits and reflective nature was especially suited to the intelligent use of pictures and symbols. Western Christians are therefore at a bit of a disadvantage compared to ancient Israel, but with some training we can become more adept at interpreting and understanding the types.

Let's work through some examples of typology in the Psalms. Perhaps the most obvious type is the nation of Israel. Why should twenty-first-century Christians sing about faraway ancient Israel in our worship songs? It seems ridiculous; and, without typology, it is! However, when we understand Old Testament Israel as a type of the New Testament church, a big-picture painting of God's kingdom on earth, then we can sing the Psalms with new understanding and relevance. It's not just that the church is given the same names as Israel was given in the Old Testament (Exod. 19:5, 6; 1 Pet. 2:9), it's that God designed Israel's history and experiences to be a mirror of the church's experiences (1 Cor. 10:6, 11). Therefore, when we sing the long historical psalms about Israel's history (Psa. 105; 106), or we sing about God's protection of Israel (121), or we sing about going up to Jerusalem to worship (121), we might have the images of Israel or Jerusalem in our minds and their names on our lips, but we are singing about Christ's New Testament church in our hearts.

Another common type in the Psalms is King David himself, the author of about half of the Psalms. Numerous psalms record David's experiences, his sufferings, his successes, his disappointments, his betrayal, his kingdom, and his reign. On the face of it, again, it seems odd to be singing about an ancient king in a foreign land if we live in London, New York, or anywhere but Israel for that matter.

If these were just old folk songs or religious songs, then I'd be the first to say they should never be sung in our worship services. Sure, they are of some historical value, but of limited spiritual value.

However, if we view King David as a type of Christ, as a prophetic picture of Christ's person and work, then we instantly connect with them, and they with us. It's not just that the New Testament tells us that Jesus was the fulfilment of the prediction of a future Son of David who would become the ultimate Davidic King. It's also that God in his providence arranged David's life so that he experienced many things the future Messianic King would also experience, though in a much greater way. By David's stories the ideal king of Israel was described. David's story was a small picture of Christ's story. Thus, God inspired David to write songs about David's own experience insofar as it mirrored and predicted the future Messiah. Thus, when we sing about David and his experiences, we are singing about Christ and his experience.

One final example of typology, this time of opposition to Christ's kingdom. The psalmist often sings about the enemies of Israel, sometimes celebrating their defeat and other times praying for it. Again, we wonder, why should I sing about that? Why not at least sing about more recent examples of our own nations defeating enemies? Well, because the psalmists saw that God designed these enemies as types, as prophetic pictures of all Christ's enemies and their ultimate fate. Thus we can sing of Og, king of Bashan, and Sihon, king of the Amorites (Psa. 135:11; 136:19, 20), while thinking about secular atheistic humanism or any number of the false religions and ideologies that threaten the cause of Christ today.

With a bit of teaching and a bit of practice, we will get better at identifying and understanding the pictures God has painted in the Psalms. Eventually it will become more instinctive and natural for us to think of the cross when we sing of sacrifice (Psa. 118:27), of Christ's blood when we sing of being purged with hyssop (51:7), of prayer when we sing of incense (141:2), and of the devil when we sing of a dangerous lion (10:9; 17:12).

Metaphor

Hebrew poetry is also rich in metaphor. A metaphor is a figure of speech that describes an object or action in a way that isn't literally true but helps explain an idea or make a comparison. For example, a teen might say, 'My home is a prison.' She is not saying that she lives in a literal prison but is complaining that it feels like that because her parents don't let her go out every night of the week. I might say of someone, 'He's a night owl.' That doesn't mean that he has big round eyes and feathery wings instead of arms. It means that he likes talking or working through the night. That kind of picture language is everywhere in the Psalms. To get the most out of these pictures, we need to pause and think about the image. We need to use our imagination to get at the core truths the picture is intended to communicate. If we do so, we will learn far more from the picture than from the few words used to describe it.

Think, for example, of a number of metaphors to describe God. The most familiar one is that God is a Shepherd (Psa. 23:1; 80:1). This tells us so much about God. Like a shepherd, God is patient with his sheep, knows his sheep, values his sheep, loves his sheep, observes his sheep, feeds his sheep, leads his sheep, pursues his sheep, rests his sheep, perseveres with his sheep. As an aside, it also tells us a lot about ourselves. Like sheep, we are foolish, slow to learn, demanding, stubborn, straying, unpredictable, restless, and dependent on our Shepherd. Do you see how just a few minutes looking at this word-picture produces so much rich theology!

Think about God pictured as the sun (Psa. 84:11). When I come across an image like that, I might look up an encyclopaedia to find out a bit more about the sun and how it teaches us about God.

- *He is hot*: Just as the sun consumes anything that touches it, so our God is a consuming fire (Heb. 12:29).
- *He is huge*: The sun's radius is over 400,000 miles: that's a hundred times greater than the earth. It is estimated to weigh 300,000 times more than the earth. That's mind-blowingly huge, as is God.
- *He is high*: The sun is ninety-two million miles from the earth, and is the centre of the galaxy, around which everything else revolves. The Lord God is the Most High, the centre of all, the pivot of all.
- *He is here*: Although the sun is so high above us, yet we can feel its effects in our daily lives. Similarly, although God is Most High, he is also most near.

- *He heals*: The sun is the source of virtually all of the earth's energy. Without the sun, everything would wither and die. Similarly, God is the source of all our spiritual energy and life.
- *He gives happiness*: When we move further from the sun, we experience darkness and depression. When the sun comes out everyone feels happier. So with God, nearness to him is joy.

Here are a few others to think about:

- God is a shield (Psa. 3:3; 28:7; 119:114), a rock (18:2; 42:9; 95:11), a fortress (31:3; 71:3).
- The Christian is like a tree (1:3), a lonely bird (102:7), grass (103:15).
- The wicked are snakes (140:3), wild animals (22:12, 13, 16), a flood (124:11), hunters (10:9).
- God's word is a lamp (119:105), gold (19:10), honey (119:103).

There are many more rich images to discover and explore in the Psalms. Keep your eyes open and set your slumbering imagination to work on these divine paintings of eternal truth.

7

Feeling the Psalms[1]

Despite hundreds of new Christian songs of every possible genre being composed every year, the ancient psalms continue to occupy a significant place in the worship diet of many Christians. Why should this be? What explains their enduring appeal?

I believe the main reason is their therapeutic value; in a day of so many disordered emotions, worshippers are discovering how the Psalms minister so powerfully to their emotional lives. I hope you can begin to experience Psalm therapy as we explore some of the emotional benefits of the Psalms.

The Psalms express the full range of human emotions
The Psalms contain such a mixture of extreme and varied emotions. As you use the Psalms, look out for these contrasting emotions: grief and joy, doubt and assurance, loneliness and fellowship, love and hate, despair and

---

[1] Adapted from David Murray, 'Therapeutic Praise,' *Tabletalk Magazine* (Orlando: Ligonier Ministries, 2012).

hope, fear and courage, failure and success, complaint and praise, shame and honour, questioning and answering, despairing and hoping, sinking and soaring, danger and deliverance, regret and gratitude, suffering and healing, guilt and forgiveness, humiliation and exultation, delight and discouragement.

Is it any wonder that Calvin called the Psalms 'an anatomy of all parts of the soul: for there is not an emotion of which anyone can be conscious that is not here represented as in a mirror. Or rather, the Holy Spirit has here drawn to life all the griefs, sorrows, fears, doubts, hopes, cares, perplexities, in short, all the distracting emotions with which the minds of men are wont to be agitated.'[1] Whatever else the Psalms tell us about the Christian life, it is that it's a life of rich and diverse feelings.

The Psalms present a realistic portrayal of the Christian life

Do your worship songs match your life? As you sing them, do they connect with your daily experience as a Christian in this world? Or do they jar with reality? Do they feel idealistic, artificial, and superficial? Do you leave worship services deeply discouraged, thinking there is something wrong with you because the songs you sang portrayed the Christian life as victory upon victory, as high after high, as joy upon joy, and your life looks very different to that? If so, turn to the Psalms, and you will find something very

---

[1] John Calvin, 'Psalms' in *Calvin's Commentaries*, trans. Henry Beveridge (Grand Rapids: Baker Book House, 1996), xxvii.

different. You will find an honest and realistic portrayal of the often raw and painful reality of the Christian life.

Sometimes the psalmist's transparency about the struggles and strife of life is initially shocking and jarring. 'Wow,' we think, 'Did he really experience that? And did he just say that to God in a worship song?' But after the initial impact, we nod our heads: 'Yes, that's me too. That's just like my life. That totally connects with me.' What a relief to encounter real life and real people and real feelings in a worship song. What a blessing to find kindred spirits who helpfully express what we often think, feel, and experience in our messy daily lives. They help us to 'get real' with ourselves, with others, and with God.

But it's not all doom and gloom either. There are also numerous psalms of confidence, hope, and optimism, which can be equally shocking in a world so full of depressing pessimism and nihilism. 'Yes,' we exclaim, 'I can sing songs of joy and assurance as a protest against the spirit of the age, and even the spirit of defeatism that often plagues the church and the Christian.' These psalms call us away from the imbalanced false piety that glories in defeat, doubt, and despair. Most of the lament psalms end with declarations of confidence, and the overall theme of the Psalms is that of festive doxology.

The Psalms contain an inspired balance between the objective and the subjective

Many contemporary praise songs tend to err on the side of the subjective experience of the worshipper. They are all about my feelings, my experience, and my moods. Some songwriters have overreacted to this and their songs are full of theology, packed with objective facts about God, but they have little engagement with or relation to the worshipper's heart and soul. They are more like sermons set to music. The overly subjective songs detach us from God. The overly objective songs detach us from ourselves. But do we have to choose between two extremes, between feelings or facts? Can't we combine them in a way that joins both together in the right proportions?

That's what the Psalms do; they strike the right balance, an 'inspired' balance between divine revelation and human emotion, between doxological theology and theological doxology. They combine the objective with the subjective in perfect proportions. They state many facts about God; but this is always with a view to stirring up our hearts and drawing us into rich communion with God. They express many feelings; but they use these feelings to draw us into contemplation of who God is. Praise is therefore rational and emotional, objective and subjective, including facts and feelings, involving mind and heart.

The Psalms open a welcome outlet for our emotions

As any counsellor will tell you, attempting to suppress all our emotions is dangerous and damaging. It harms not just our psychology and our spirituality but even our bodies. The stoical stifling and shutting down of feeling creates an inner pressure and stress that eventually takes a toll on our nervous system, our body chemistry, and our major organs. Of course, some counsellors try to solve this by encouraging 'venting' where the one being counselled is told to just 'let rip … to let it all hang out … to take the lid off and remove all restraint.' This may give some temporary relief, but it doesn't last and it often adds to the problems because of the sinful expressions that are usually involved.

Churches and Christians can also fall into similar traps, with some squashing and stifling emotions while others enable the 'let it all hang out' school of thought. Neither approach is healthy, nor are they found in the Psalms. Instead, the Psalms open the pressure valve of our hearts; they encourage us to lift the lid of our souls and be transparent and authentic. But they also direct us in how to express and articulate our emotions. We don't need to bottle them up or deny them. Instead God has inspired songs to admit them, let them out, and reach up to God with them. What a relief! I can sing what's really on my mind and heart, and God provides me with words to rightly describe and convey these emotions. The Psalms reach in to find these emotions and then reach upwards to God with them using words and emotions that we know he approves of and accepts. We can feel deeply and openly, be it exuberant joy, raging against injustice, angst about God's providence, or the desolation of depression. The Psalms also call us to a deeper, higher, and wider emotional life. Through them God is calling us away from one-dimensional black-and-white spirituality to a Dolby Stereo HD version we can enjoy.

The Psalms call for the transformation of our emotions

The Psalms not only allow us to feel and express our emotions in a legitimate way, which is its own therapy; they also call for their transformation. The Psalms let us put all our feelings on the table, but they also help us sort them out, challenge them, and even change them. By articulating our emotions—describing them, putting words to them—we are enabled to see them more clearly, discern whether they are appropriate or not, understand where they are coming from, discover their roots, identify any falsehoods that are driving them, and find the truths of God that will begin to heal and help them.

In the next chapter we will look at an example of how God transforms depression to hope using his word and works, but look for other examples of emotional therapy like this in the Psalms. Some start with anger, others with self-pity, still others with fear-filled unbelief. But in the course of the psalm these feelings are shaped, trimmed, and moulded by God's word and works to leave us better rather than worse. Angry rebellion is changed into peaceful submission, self-pity is shaped into God-centred confidence, and fear is moulded into courage. And this is all done in such a way that God is exalted and worshipped throughout. There's not an emotion in the world that you can feel which is not addressed by the Psalms, changed by the Psalms, and turned into worship by the Psalms.

The Psalms summon us to sympathetic emotion

As a rebellious teenager, I often sat in my Psalm-singing church wondering why I was singing words that had no relevance to me whatsoever. Why sing about doubt, when I had none? Why sing about sorrow, when I was perfectly happy? Or, some Sundays, why sing about joy when I felt so depressed about my life? Give me songs that mean something to me!

Well, of course, such is the mindset of a self-centred teenager. All I could think about was I, me, and myself. But when God started working in my soul I started to see a bit further than my own nose. Lo and behold, there were other people in church, and, even more surprisingly, they seemed to be resonating with the songs. As I began to grow in faith and actually start talking to other Christians, I realized that while I may not have been feeling the emotions of the Psalms, others certainly did. My singing slowly changed from being a self-focused activity to a group activity. When I sang about depression, I remembered the depressed young woman I spoke to a couple of weeks before and I thought about her more, and felt for her more.

The Psalms taught me to weep with those who weep and to rejoice with those who rejoice, no matter if I felt exactly the opposite. They reminded me of the emotional diversity of the body of Christ and invited me to share in the sufferings and successes of others. They turned me inside out.

The Psalms provide an emotional stimulus to ethical faithfulness

I've been trying to emphasize the vital role of emotional engagement and stimulus in the Psalms. However, unlike so many modern songs that result in only temporary emotional stimulation, the Psalms also call us to practical obedience. The root meaning of emotion is 'to move someone or something.' Emotion is therefore intended to produce movement or action. For example, God does not just call us to joy for joy's sake, but because the joy of the Lord is our strength (Neh. 8:10). Joy strengthens us for service. The emotional energy of happiness stirs up physical energy and zeal for service and obedience. Emotional theology must result in practical theology.

We often hear people saying, 'I need to go to therapy.' That may be so, but why not try Psalm therapy first? And even if you do need professional therapy, would you not also benefit from Psalm therapy alongside? And for those of us who don't need therapy, don't you think the Psalms could still have therapeutic value for you in teaching you how to feel and express your emotions in ways that will bless you and all those around you?

8

Counselling with the Psalms

'But I'm not a counsellor. So I might as well skip to the next chapter.'

Wait, wait! At the very least, you are counselling yourself. It's something we all do all the time. We tell ourselves stories about ourselves, an inner narrative that has a huge influence on our thoughts, feelings, words, and actions. Sometimes the stories are accurate and helpful. Other times they are false and harmful. What if I told you that the Psalms can help change your inner narrative so that your self-counselling, your inner story, is helpful rather than harmful? Does that interest you?

Although you may not realize it, you are probably doing informal counselling all the time. You listen to friends and families as they tell their stories to you. They share their thoughts about themselves and their lives and you try to process what they are saying and respond with words that will help them. You search your own wisdom reserves from your experience of the world, as well as God's wisdom reserves in his word, and you attempt to speak into their lives in a way that improves them. That's counselling! So we all do it, although often informally and unintentionally. Wouldn't you like a bit of formal training in this so that you can do it more intentionally and effectively? That's where this chapter on counselling with the Psalms comes in. So stick with me.

Where should we start? Well, we could really start anywhere. Psalm 1, for example, could be used to counsel someone towards better friend and media choices. Psalms 3 and 4 counsel insomniacs how to enjoy trustful sleep even in the midst of their enemies. Psalm 8 counsels the young and the weak to take courage from God's power evidenced in creation in order to speak truth to God's enemies. Psalm 16 counsels the dying to hope in the blessings of heavenly life after death and ultimately to hope for the resurrection of their body. I could go on and on.

But for the purposes of this chapter, instead of giving a brief summary of the counselling lessons from numerous psalms, I thought it would be best to just choose one psalm and go deeper, to use it as a detailed example of how to use the Psalms in counselling. I've selected Psalm 77 because it's the psalm that I've used most in counselling people with depression. Although there may be other elements involved in healing depression (*e.g.* medication, exercise, diet, sleep, fellowship), I've found that there's always a need for re-training thinking patterns and that Psalm 77 provides an ideal template for that.

Emotional elephants

In *The Coddling of the American Mind: How Good Intentions and Bad Ideas are Setting up a Generation for Failure*, authors Jonathan Haidt and Greg Lukianof identify 'Three Great Untruths' that have spread widely in recent years, mainly through the educational system. These three great untruths have led to widespread and deep emotional problems such as soaring rates of teen anxiety, depression, and suicide.

The second of these great untruths is the untruth of emotional reasoning, more popularly known as 'Always trust your feelings.' Emotional reasoning is the cognitive distortion that occurs when we interpret what's happening in ways that are consistent with our emotions rather than investigating what's true.

The authors of *The Coddling of the American Mind* illustrate this problem by asking us to imagine a small rider on top of a large elephant. To simplify, the small rider is our reason and the large elephant is our emotions. Problems arise when we let our emotions drive our reason. Letting an elephant loose in our life or in public is not a good policy for peace and rest! What's needed is to restore the primacy of reason, to give reason the reins of our emotions, and to train reason how to control our emotions.

I believe these authors are largely correct in this part of their analysis of our culture and of human nature. It's surprisingly in line with much of what the Bible teaches. However, I believe that their solution, while along the right lines, is incomplete and inadequate. It will bring a degree of control and rest to our emotions, but I believe that God can give deeper, longer, and more satisfying emotional rest.

Where are they right? First, they diagnose the problem and consequences of letting the elephant of our emotions control our lives. Second, they identify the strengthening of reason as the key to getting our emotions under control and at rest. This is consistent with biblical anthropology and much good can come from this approach to the emotions. However, the Bible goes further by diagnosing reason as also fallen and flawed. It needs to be enlightened; it needs truth from outside the human mind.

If we go back to our illustration, we see the rider of reason doing his best to rein in the elephant and point it in the right direction. However, if we look more closely, the rider's eyes are squinting and struggling to see the way ahead. He has a vision problem. He needs glasses, spectacles, to be able to see the road signs. That's where the word of God comes in. It supplies clarity of vision to see the road signs and plot the safest route ahead, and also points us to the right final destination.

But even more than that is required: the rider needs his heart changed, because he doesn't like what he sees on the signs. He thinks he can do without the spectacles. He needs faith to trust the spectacles, especially when what they show contradicts what he thinks. So, more is needed than getting reason into the driving seat. We need a biblically informed reason that submits to and trusts what the Bible teaches us.

Psalm 77 therapy

That's what we see in Psalm 77. In the first half of the psalm (verses 1-9), we see a believer whose emotions are in control, causing him terrible distress and stress. It's someone far from emotional rest. But by the end of the psalm we see someone at peace, someone whose emotions are under the control of biblical reason, and whose emotions are therefore nurturing and nourishing his life rather than upsetting and upending it. We want to follow the process outlined in this psalm in order to apply it to our own lives.

Before we do so, a word of qualification. There are people, believers included, who suffer with clinical depression or anxiety or other emotional disorders. While Psalm 77 therapy may play a role in their recovery, they will usually need more than this. They may need to consult their doctor and address physical issues that are contributing to their emotional disturbance. There are also other issues that may need to be addressed such as diet, exercise, sleep, relaxation, etc. But, here we want to focus on this reason-versus-emotions battle, and we will do so by asking two questions: *How did I get into this mood?* and, *How do I get out of this mood?*

Identifying false thoughts: how did I get into this mood?

This question will help us recognize when emotions are in control and identify which false beliefs are strengthening the elephant. We will do so by noticing three phases in the process: Facts, Feelings, and Thoughts.

Distressing facts

Asaph's life situation is not defined in detail but is described as 'the day of my trouble' (verse 2). This is a general description that covers a multitude of possibilities and therefore allows us to apply his thoughts to multiple possible troubles.

Distressing feelings

1. He feels helpless and is crying out (verse 1).

2. He feels sad and depressed, as evidenced by his endless weeping and inconsolable distress (verse 2).

3. He feels troubled when he thinks about God (verse 3).

4. He feels discontented, as evidenced by his complaints (verse 3).

5. He feels overwhelmed in his spirit (verse 3).

6. He feels so anxious that he cannot sleep and feels so stressed that he cannot speak (verse 4).

7. He feels nostalgia for the past (verse 5).

8. He feels abandoned, unloved, and forgotten by God (verses 7-9).

The emotional tone is one of pessimistic despair and depression.

Distressing thoughts

Asaph's emotions are first, front, and centre. They are in control and are dictating and guiding his thoughts. Distressing trouble leads to distressing feelings which lead to distressing thoughts. These include:

1. He thinks about God and is troubled (verse 3).

2. He thinks it's God that's keeping him awake (verse 4).

3. He thinks that the past was all great but the future is all bleak (verses 5-7).

4. He thinks God has abandoned him forever (verse 7).

5. He thinks that God will never love him or show him favour again (verse 7).

6. He thinks that God's character has changed from merciful and gracious to simply just and angry (verses 6, 7).

7. He thinks that God has broken his promises (verse 8).

8. He thinks God has forgotten to deal with him in grace and has shut the door on his mercy (verse 7).

Distressing facts lead to distressing feelings which produce distressing thoughts. His distressed emotions are producing a number of cognitive distortions which in turn produce more distressing feelings. It's a kind of negative feedback loop which feeds on itself, no matter whether we start with emotions or thoughts. Irrational thoughts lead to negative feelings that motivate reasoning to find evidence in support of negative beliefs.

How do we free ourselves from this vicious circle? How do we put fact-based reasoning in control of the elephant that's doing so much damage? That's the question we now turn to by looking at verses 10-20 of Psalm 77.

Challenging false thoughts: how do I get out of this mood?

We need to challenge and change false thinking with the truth, with biblical thinking.

Distressing facts

There is no evidence that Asaph could change the facts or that his situation changed. His situation and circumstances do not change. His external world does not change. But his internal world undergoes a revolution. And the biggest change is that he begins with his thoughts, not his feelings. He lets his thoughts direct his feelings rather than the other way around.

Believing thoughts

The first thing he does is pause. 'Selah' at the end of verse 9 indicates that he takes time out from his rumination. He pauses, stills his soul, calms down, and this creates a buffer for him to decompress, unwind, and create space and silence for new thoughts to form that transform his perspective and outlook.

He looks back on the previous cycle and where it took him and says, 'This is my infirmity' (verse 10 KJV).[1] He expresses disapproval of how he's been processing his circumstances, how he's been reacting to events. It's a confession that amounts to 'This way of thinking and the subsequent feelings are a weakness of mine. This is not something I'm proud of. It's something that has hurt me and I need to change.'

So, what does he do? By God's grace, he begins to force himself to think new thoughts, to search out and explore new areas for study and meditation (verse 10). Notice

---

[1] The NKJV translation is 'This is my anguish,' and in the ESV 'I will appeal to this.' In this case, I believe the KJV gets closest to the original Hebrew.

all the cognitive verbs: 'I will remember' occurs twice in verse 11. Also, 'I will ponder,' and 'I will meditate' (verse 12). Reason is beginning to assert itself; thinking is rising and strengthening in his life, displacing the emotions from supreme control.

But notice what he's going to think about. He's going to think truths about God. He can't change the facts of his life, but he can add to these facts in his thinking. He can add biblical and theological facts. So he starts thinking about objective truth from the Bible.

1. *I will appeal to this, to the years of the right hand of the Most High* (verse 10). The Most High was the name Abraham gave to God after a notable victory (Gen. 14:22). This seems to be a reference to Christ, who sits at the right hand of the Most High, and especially to his years, which may be a reference to his eternity, his foreverness.

2. *I will remember the deeds of the Lord ... your wonders of old ... all your work ... your mighty deeds* (verses 10-12). He is now looking at God's redemptive acts in time and letting them fill his mind and mouth.

3. He focuses on God's strength and might on behalf of his people (verses 13, 14).

4. He is especially thinking about God's redemption of his people from Egypt, the Red Sea deliverance where God showed his superiority over all natural and human powers (verses 15-19).

5. He then remembers God's shepherding of his people through the wilderness by Moses and Aaron's leadership (verses 19, 20).

What a difference in his thoughts! No more looking back negatively and nostalgically, but looking back positively and believingly. No more looking at what he had lost, but at what was still his, and for him, in God's redemptive acts. The implicit idea is that God has not changed, that God's promises are still trustworthy, that God is still involved in his life, and is guarding him and guiding him through his own wilderness.

As God's true redemptive character and acts come into the foreground, Asaph's trouble recedes into the background. By the end of the psalm the pervasive 'I' of the first half of the psalm has disappeared and the objective facts of faith have captured all his attention. Also, he is no longer talking *about* God *negatively*, but talking *to* God and worshipping God *positively*.

Stable feelings

Reason—biblical reason, believing reason—is now in control, and the result is a significant stabilizing of his emotions. It's not stated explicitly, but it's clearly implied that along with the believing thoughts come stable feelings. There's a very different tone in his voice. The emotional temperature is quite different from verse 10 onwards. Instead of doubt there is confidence; instead of pessimism there is optimism; instead of vulnerability there is security; instead of distress there is comfort; instead of confusion there is clarity.

The facts of his life have not changed, but his feelings have, because, with the help of God's word and works, he has changed his thoughts about these facts. We can see similar patterns of spiritual and emotional therapy in Psalms 42 and 43, Job 19, and Habakkuk 3.

The key is to identify which specific thoughts drive particular emotions. For example, if I constantly think about losses, I'll be sad. If I think about sin all the time, I'll feel guilty. If I always think I'm too thin or too fat, I'll feel embarrassed. But if I think about God's gifts, I'll be thankful; if I think about God's beauty, I'll be inspired; if I think about God's sovereignty, I'll feel peaceful. Develop an ability to challenge and change your thoughts, beliefs, and emotions by using this biblical pattern. You'll notice that it's not just your thoughts that are transformed but your words and actions too.

Just positive thinking?

Some might say 'This is just self-hypnosis,' or 'This is just "the art of positive thinking."' No, it's quite different. Neither I nor the psalmist are advocating that you lie to yourself or deceive yourself or deny reality. Rather, this is about telling the truth to yourself and getting back in touch with ultimate reality. It does not deny painful facts about our lives. But it does challenge false thoughts, exaggerated thoughts, and excessive thoughts about ourselves. And it does urge the addition of spiritual realities to our thought patterns, truths about God that must be held firmly and constantly before us if we are to avoid both false negativity and false positivity and get to true reality.

Use these steps to counsel yourself and begin to notice the difference that Asaph did. Then, perhaps try to help someone in your family or circle of friends by taking them through this psalm. Remember, this is not usually a cure-all for severe depression, but part of a holistic package of care that can contribute significantly to healing. Neither am I saying that this is 'once and done.' You usually have to repeat this again and again to really change deeply ingrained thought-patterns. But remember, you don't have to call yourself a counsellor to counsel God's truth into your own or others' lives.[1]

[1] For more on how to use the Bible to re-train our thinking, see Chris Williams, et al, *I'm Not Supposed to Feel Like This: A Christian Approach to Coping with Depression and Anxiety* (London: Hodder & Stoughton, 2002).

9

Witnessing in the Psalms

You might think the Psalms were written exclusively for a tiny little nation and her people, and that they had and have no relevance to others. In this chapter, I want to show you how the Psalms were actually intended as part of Israel's witness to the world and to remind Israel of her calling as a missionary to the world. In doing so, we will see how much the Psalms have to teach us about our own duties of evangelism and mission.

Although Israel developed over time into a proud, isolationist nation, marked by haughty nationalism and contempt for non-Israelites, that was not God's original intention or calling for Israel. Rather he called her to be a blessing to the world. We see hints of that in God's covenant with Abraham, the father of Israel, where God promised to use Abraham and his seed to bless all the nations of the earth (Gen. 12:3). In this covenant, God narrowed his covenantal focus to the descendants of Abraham in order to secure the eventual arrival of the Messiah. But it was a narrowing with a view to widening.

We see it even more clearly when God constituted Israel as a nation and promised to make Israel a 'kingdom of priests and a holy nation' (Exod. 19:6). Insofar as Israel held to God's covenant precepts, she would be holy and useful to God. Her usefulness is summed up as being a priestly kingdom, meaning that God would use this nation as a mediator to the nations, as his channel or pipeline of blessing to the world. What a calling!

Israel's history, however, reveals how badly the nation failed in this calling. Not only did they become an unholy nation, they blocked up God's channel of blessing to the nations of the world and refused to reach out with God's message of salvation to the Gentiles. Jonah's story is a personalized narrative of what was true of them on a national level. Having been called to be a witness to the nations, Israel disobeyed and was punished for it with the dark and deep exile they experienced in Babylon. While this exile cured Israel of their idolatry, it still didn't cure them of their nationalistic pride and exclusivism. This is demonstrated especially in their opposition to Jesus' message of Gentile inclusion (Luke 4:25-29). Even his apostles sometimes fell into this error (Gal. 2:11), despite Christ's command to go out into all the world and make disciples (Matt. 28:18-20).

One of the ways God reminded Israel of their calling to be his witness in and to the world was through their singing of the Psalms. They didn't just have the ancient covenant documents but living singing of the Psalms to remind them of their missionary calling and duty. Let's look then at the

Psalms and the varied ways in which God called Israel and calls us to be his witnesses in the world.

The witness of the individual

Worldwide witness begins with personal witnessing. There's no point in going out to the nations with the gospel unless you have first believed it and experienced it for yourself. Thus, in Psalms 40:1-3, we read:

> *I waited patiently for the Lord;*
> > *he inclined to me, and heard my cry.*
> *He drew me up from the pit of destruction,*
> > *out of the miry bog,*
> > *and set my feet upon a rock,*
> > *making my steps secure.*
> *He put a new song in my mouth,*
> > *a song of praise to our God.*
> *Many will see and fear,*
> > *and put their trust in the Lord.*

This is one of many personal testimonies in the Psalms, descriptions of how God sovereignly, powerfully, and graciously saved and forgave needy sinners, resulting in them proclaiming God's salvation to all who would hear of it (Psa. 51:13, 15). The psalmist calls out to others to come and hear him tell what God did for his soul (66:16).

The witness of the family

Psalm 101 is sometimes described as the 'House-warming Psalm.' Some Jews sing it when they buy a new home. They go through the house singing the psalm in each room.

When you read the psalm, you can understand why. It describes the kind of home they wanted to set up, a home that would be characterized by holiness: holy eyes, holy ears, holy tongues, holy friends, and holy justice.

The family is also the setting for passing on the stories of Israel's history and God's revelation. Psalm 78 is one of a number of 'historical psalms' in which the parents are concerned to pass on to subsequent generations all that the Lord has done for them. The family has a major part to play in God's plan of maintaining his truth and the witness to it in the world (Psa. 127; 128). The psalmist's prayer is that God would continue to raise up future generations that would keep alive this testimony for subsequent generations (90:16, 17; 102:18, 28; 145:4).

The witness of the church
The psalmists do not confine their witness to the individual and the family. Rather they see the public worship of God as a place to also testify to God's works, word, and worth (Psa. 40:9, 10). They want to share what God has done, what God has said, and what God is with other believers (22:25; 26:12; 89:5). When we eavesdrop on a congregation of Israelites, we hear the sweet melody of salvation songs (89:15). God's beauty is declared there and enjoyed there (27:4).

The witness of the nation
Because the kingdom was such an important element of Israel's witness to the outside world, it was imperative that the nation be a holy nation. This explains why there was so

much concern in the Psalms for the purity of the nation and its leaders, especially the administration of justice by its judges and kings. God expresses his desire for justice and his abhorrence of injustice in the Psalms, especially favouritism towards the rich and powerful and the neglect and abuse of the weak, the poor, widows and orphans. For God, the pursuit of justice was not an optional extra but an essential foundation for Israel's witness. Thus God, through the Psalms, challenges the nation's leaders to do justice and to remember that they will one day be judged by him (Psa. 82). Israel is reminded of the blessing of being God's special people and of having God as their God (33:12). That's not a blessing they are to keep to themselves.

The witness to the nations

Having laid this foundation of personal, family, ecclesiastical, and national witness, we now return to Israel's witness to the nations. The more people were faithful in these other areas of witness, the more effective the nation's witness was to the nations of the world. The holier Israel was, the more effective the nation was as a kingdom of priests. Unholiness blocks the pipe of blessing to the world.

God designed the Psalms to remind Israel of his authority over the nations, his ownership claim of them, and their duty to pay allegiance to him (Psa. 2; 9:17). The kingdoms are the Lord's and he rules over them (22:28). He is good to all peoples, not just Israel (145:9). As such, all nations and peoples are exhorted to praise God (117:1; 148:11). The Psalms also reminded Israel of their obligation to declare

God's glory among the nations and his great and gracious deeds among all peoples (96:3). How can they know about God and their duties to him if they do not hear his word?

In addition to these reminders of God's authority over the nations, his goodness to them, the debt of praise they owe to him, and Israel's obligation to spread God's message, Israel was also given prayers for blessing upon the nations. Israel was to pray for God's way and God's saving health to be known among the nations (67:2) and is assured that this would result in joyful songs by the nations (67:4, 5).

One of the missionary strategies Israel was to employ in persuading the nations was to call the nations to compare their gods with the one true God of Israel. They were to put their idols beside the God of Israel and make a decision about who was most worthy of worship. The God of Israel is not afraid of a competition with false gods. Go on, say the Psalms, compare the helplessness of your god with our almighty God (96:4, 5; 115:3-9).

The Psalms remind Israel that their witness to the nations has met with some success and will meet with even more as they obey their divine commission more (Psa. 65:5). The nations already see his glory (19:1-3; 97:6), his righteousness, and salvation (98:2, 3). The psalmist expressed confidence that he will sing God's praises among the nations (57:9; 108:3). Many times the Psalms prophesy that even the nations at the ends of the world will turn to the Lord and all kinds of peoples shall worship God (9:20). All kings and nations will bow down and serve him (72:11), and all nations shall call him blessed (72:17; 86:9, 10). Some of the most unlikely nations will bring forth fruit to God (68:31; 87:4). Many kings will bring tribute to him (68:29; 72:10, 11). He will be exalted in and among the nations of the earth (46:10).

However, it's not all encouragement; there are also warnings. Psalm 2 calls the unrepentant kings and people to be wise and listen to divine instruction or perish in his anger (Psa. 2:10). All the nations that reject God will be turned into hell (9:17). The rebel nations will eventually be subdued under Christ's feet (47:3).

Just as the Psalms were sung to remind Israel of her missionary obligation, to stimulate missionary prayers, to raise expectations of gospel success, and to motivate missionary words and actions, so they can do for us today. God's New Testament people are still called to be a holy nation, a kingdom of priests (1 Pet. 2:9; Rev. 1:6). We too have a tendency to be inward-looking, individualistic, proud, and pharisaical to those outside the church, and therefore need the Psalms to re-orient us and encourage us in local evangelism and international missions. Let's pray the words of Psalm 67 together:

> *May God be gracious to us and bless us*
> *and make his face to shine upon us,   Selah*
> *that your way may be known on earth,*
> *your saving power among all nations.*
> *Let the peoples praise you, O God;*
> *let all the peoples praise you!*
> *Let the nations be glad and sing for joy,*
> *for you judge the peoples with equity*

    and guide the nations upon earth.   Selah.
Let the peoples praise you, O God;
    let all the peoples praise you!
The earth has yielded its increase;
    God, our God, shall bless us.
God shall bless us;
    let all the ends of the earth fear him!

10

Blessing in the Psalms

'Lord, bless Dad. Bless Grandma. Bless me. Bless the church.' How many times have you prayed such prayers? How many times did you know what you were praying for? What does 'bless' mean?

We wish one another 'God bless' and we talk about being #blessed. But what do we mean? 'Bless,' 'blessing,' and 'blessed' are some of the most used Christian words and some of the least understood. I want to put that right in this chapter which explores 'blessing' in the Psalms.

The first thing to notice is that 'blessed' is the first word in the first psalm, and the first psalm concentrates on what it means to be blessed or cursed. Second, 'bless,' 'blessing,' or 'blessed' occur one hundred and two times in the Psalms. It's not only the book's first theme but its constant theme and perhaps its most important theme.

What then does it mean to be blessed or to wish blessing upon someone? Some theologians have tried to equate 'blessed' with happy. Welsh preacher Martyn Lloyd-Jones, for example, began his commentary on Psalm 1 with these words:

> So the first thing the Bible tells us is that happiness is possible. And I emphasize that because this is the most staggering, the most surprising thing of all in a world like this; but it is the great message of the Bible. It comes to us as we are, and it says, 'Happiness, blessedness, is possible.'[1]

In his well-researched book on happiness, American author Randy Alcorn also argued that in the Bible, joy, blessing, and happiness are all synonyms, different words for the same thing.

Others have gone to great lengths to distinguish blessedness from happiness, asserting that the former is an objective position before God and the latter is a subjective experience in the human emotions.

The blessedness contained in the Psalms is more complex than an either/or choice between the objective and the subjective. It certainly contains a large objective component because, when God pronounces a person blessed, he is pronouncing his favour towards and approval of a person. That's where blessing starts, but it doesn't end there. It often contains much subjective happiness as well. Not always, but often, the experience of being blessed by God carries with it great human happiness. Surely that's the message of Psalm 1. That man or woman is truly blessed who possesses both the favour of God and human happiness both in this world and the next.

[1] Dr Martyn Lloyd-Jones, *True Happiness: An Exposition of Psalm One* (Bryntirion: Gwasg Bryntirion Press, 1997), p. 12.

That's one of the great themes of the Psalms. Walking in God's path and obeying God's word brings great blessing into a person's life. Faith and faithfulness is usually the way to God's favour and personal happiness. However, that is not always the case. It is generally true, but there are exceptions. It's helpful to pause here and distinguish between two kinds of wisdom in the Psalms, practical and philosophical wisdom.

Practical wisdom

Practical wisdom, sometimes called 'didactic' or 'lower' wisdom, promises blessings on right living (*e.g.* Psa. 1; 15) and is also found frequently in the book of Proverbs. It was usually taught within a family context, tended to be optimistic, and was popular with common people. It often contained simple and easily memorized sayings and it was intended to help people live in wise and healthy ways. While practical wisdom was generally true, there were exceptions to the general rules. That's where philosophical wisdom enters.

Philosophical wisdom

This was often called 'reflective' or 'higher' wisdom and is also found in Job and Ecclesiastes. Instead of the short, sharp, pithy sayings of practical theology, philosophical wisdom tended to be lengthy discourses and monologues grappling with life's most difficult problems, such as a right view of wealth (Psa. 49), struggles with injustice (37), or painful providences in the lives of the righteous (73). It does not deny practical wisdom, but highlights how life has its enigmas and puzzles. It says that practical wisdom has its limits and must not be read in isolation from philosophical wisdom.

God's favour and human happiness

Putting this together, we can say that to be blessed by God certainly means first and foremost to enjoy God's favour and approval. That is an objective factual reality that is unaffected by whether we feel it or not. This is not speaking so much about justification, a sinner's acceptance before God. That never changes, that never fluctuates. But God's blessing can and does. He puts his blessing upon faith, obedience, and loyal service of him in this world.

Second, that blessed life will usually be accompanied by great happiness and joy. Walking in sin and disobedience is a sad and depressing life. Sure, there may be moments of short and superficial pleasure, but it always comes with a hangover or a sting in the tail. In contrast, walking in the path of blessing is the happiest way to live. God has designed his commandments so that those who obey them are choosing a way of life that God has designed to be generally happy and advantageous.

Some exceptions

Third, there are exceptions to this connection between obedience and blessing. There are times when walking in the path of obedience will be painful and involve suffering and loss. Although it is still possible to feel supernatural happiness in the midst of suffering for Christ (*e.g.* Stephen in Acts 7:55-60), that is not always the case. Sometimes a persecuted Christian can experience dreadful pain and suffering. They can see their families tortured and even killed. However, despite these subjective miseries, despite their bitter grief, they are no less blessed by God in the objective sense of being the objects of his favour and approval. Indeed, as Jesus reminded us in his beatitudes, the persecuted are even more blessed when suffering for righteousness' sake (Matt. 5:10-12). God's favour is towards them in a special way. It takes great faith to believe that. However, such faith will revive one's feelings by believing that whether or not there is a smile on my face or in my heart, God's smile is upon me, and that's enough.

Fourth, even if there is no subjective experience of happiness, and there is only faith's believing that God's blessing is upon us, the Lord will—possibly in this world, definitely in the next—restore that happiness and joy so that the path of righteousness is ultimately not only the path to God's objective favour but to an eternal happiness in heaven. There the objective favour of God and the subjective happiness of God's people will correspond exactly, perfectly, and eternally.

Blessed and blessings

So what is the blessed life and what are we praying for when we pray for blessing? Let's look at these two questions by surveying the Psalms' answers. The blessed person:

- Does not listen to ungodly counsel, follow a sinful lifestyle, or mock what is holy (Psa. 1:1).
- Delights in God's word and meditates upon it (1:2).
- Kisses the Son of God by faith (2:12).
- Considers the poor (41:1).
- Is chosen by God to worship him (65:4).
- Dwells in God's house (84:4).
- Seeks strength from God (84:5).
- Keeps God's ways in his heart (84:5).
- Trusts in God (84:12).
- Does justice and righteousness at all times (106:3).
- Fears the Lord (112:1; 128:1).
- Delights in God's commandments (112:1).
- Is undefiled by the world and walks in God's law (119:1).
- Keeps God's testimonies (119:2).
- Seeks the Lord with his whole heart (119:2).

That is the way to divine blessing. And what can we expect when we get there? A multitude of objective and subjective blessings.

- Blessed with growth and fruitfulness (1:3).
- Blessed with the shield of God's favour (5:12).
- Blessed with strength and peace (29:11).
- Blessed with forgiveness (32:1).
- Blessed with a guileless spirit (32:2).
- Blessed with trust in God (34:8).
- Blessed with inheritance of the earth (37:22).
- Blessed with trust in God and fearlessness before men (40:4).
- Blessed with long life (41:2).

- Blessed with God's smile (67:1).
- Blessed with evangelistic success (67:1).
- Blessed with a heavy load of daily benefits (68:19).
- Blessed with joyful songs (89:15).
- Blessed with the divine discipline and discipling (94:12).
- Blessed with divine provision (132:15).
- Blessed with eternal life (133:3).
- Blessed with God's favour on one's family (147:13).

So, when we pray that God would bless our family, or an individual, or ourselves, that's what we are praying for. And we are praying that they would not only arrive at the place of God's blessing but that they would follow the path of blessing to get there too.

How then do we explain the Psalms which speak of people blessing God (*e.g.* Psa. 34:1; 68:26; 113:1-3; 134:1)? Can human beings bless God? In these contexts, it probably means to express approval of God or to praise him and honour him, especially out of gratitude for blessings received.

The cursed

We cannot leave this subject without considering the opposite of divine blessing, and that is to be under God's curse. The Psalms focus largely on what it is to be blessed, but as even the opening two psalms make clear, there is another side to the story. Not everyone is blessed, because not everyone seeks the path of blessing. There are those whose lives are characterized by their cursing of God and his people (Psa. 10:7; 59:12; 62:4; 109:17, 18, 28) and therefore are cursed by God (37:22; 119:21).

To be cursed by God is be the object of God's frown and fury. God's curse is upon the person who lives a life of disobedience. That is usually a terrible, unhappy life, but there are exceptions. There are times when the wicked seem to prosper and be happy in their sin. However, such examples are rarer than we think; and however a wicked person may feel, they are objectively opposed and rejected by God. Also, even if their happiness lasts long in this world, at the end their inner state and feelings will be brought into line with their objective state before God (Psa. 37; 73). They will be cursed forever, feel cursed forever, and experience God's curse forever. The Psalms lay this out as well and make it crystal clear that there are only two options, only two ways to live in this world and the next: blessed or cursed.

11

Cursing with the Psalms[1]

If you start reading or singing the Psalms, it won't be long before you come across verses in which the psalmists seem to call for God to curse their enemies. These are often called 'imprecatory psalms' because they invoke or 'imprecate' God's judgment on people.

That's a problem, isn't it, because pleading with God to punish our enemies does appear to be contrary both to the spirit and letter of the New Testament (Matt. 5:43, 44). It's therefore no surprise that some people view these psalms as pre-Christian, sub-Christian, or simply non-Christian, and refuse to sing them. Others go further and argue that such psalms prove that the Psalms were only for Old Testament times and none of them should be sung today.

So, what do we do with the imprecatory psalms? Should we just ignore them and restrict ourselves to the 'Christian' psalms? In this chapter, I hope to show that the imprecatory

[1] Adapted from David Murray, 'Christian Cursing,' *Sing a New Song: Recovering Psalm Singing for the Twenty-First Century*, eds. Joel Beeke and Anthony Selvaggio (Grand Rapids: Reformation Heritage Books, 2010).

psalms, when rightly understood, are both Christian and suitable for Christian praise, not least because they point us to Christ our Saviour.

First, I will examine some wrong solutions to the imprecatory psalms 'problem.' Second, I will propose ten helps for Christian singing of the imprecatory psalms. Before we do this, let me briefly state the extent of the 'problem.' Three psalms are mainly imprecatory (35, 69, 109). Others have imprecatory verses (5, 7, 10, 28, 31, 40, 55, 58, 59, 70, 71, 79, 83, 137, 139, 140). It has been argued that ninety of the one hundred and fifty psalms have imprecatory language. Having said all that, it is still important to remember that imprecations are found in relatively few verses and represent but a minor theme in the Psalms. Let's start by looking at some wrong solutions to this problem.

Wrong solutions

Old Testament versus New Testament

First, some have argued that imprecatory language was fine in the Old Testament but not in the New Testament, and that these psalms are included in the Scriptures only to show the contrast between the two eras. This solution is unacceptable because it ends up with God contradicting his moral law over time. Also, the 'contrast' is not so stark as is often claimed. The Old Testament has commandments to love our enemies and turn from vengeance (Lev. 19:17, 18; Prov. 24:17, 18; 25:21, 22), while the New Testament also contains imprecations (2 Tim. 4:14), as we shall see in more detail below.

Sinful men and sinful prayers

Some have said that as these were sinful expressions on the lips of sinful men, we should not take them upon our lips. We reject this explanation because it raises questions about the inspiration of Scripture. David claimed, without qualification, that his psalms were inspired by God's Spirit (2 Sam. 23:1, 2). Also, the titles of some imprecatory psalms indicate that they were to be used in public worship (*e.g.* Psalm 69 is 'for the Chief Musician').

Demons not people

Some interpreters say that the imprecations are called upon the heads of demons, not people. We may certainly have evil spirits in view as we sing the imprecatory psalms; that would be a legitimate application. However, the New Testament tells us that the imprecations in Psalm 69:25 and 109:6-9 were also fulfilled in Judas (Acts 1:20), a real human person.

Predictions not prayers

Another common explanation is that these psalms were to be sung in the future tense and that the authors were saying what would happen in the future, rather than desiring it. They were predicting it, rather than praying it. It is certainly a truth of Scripture that God will punish the wicked; however, that is not the whole truth of the imprecatory Scriptures. These imprecations may be prophetic, but they are also prayers. In fact, some grammarians claim that the Hebrew will not allow for the future tense and a prophetic interpretation.

Exaggeration

Last, some say these imprecations are examples of hyperbolic language, or purposeful exaggeration, a figure of speech that is often used in Hebrew poetry. However, while a figurative interpretation may help us understand some imprecatory expressions such as 'break their teeth' (Psa. 58:6), we cannot deny that the imprecations possess some basic literal element of calling down God's judgment on enemies.

Ten helps

Having proposed some solutions to the common 'problems' ascribed to the imprecatory psalms, let me now suggest some helps that will improve our understanding and even motivate our singing of them.

(1) Gospel curse

First, the imprecations have their roots in the first gospel promise. The curses of the Psalms are rooted in the gospel curse on the Serpent and his seed in Genesis 3:14, 15. Moses develops this further by showing that the gospel promises contain both salvation and cursing (Gen. 12:3). In the imprecations the psalmist is basically saying, 'God, be faithful to your promise to curse those who curse your people.'

(2) David's character

Consider the general character of David, the author of most of the imprecatory psalms. The biblical narratives and the Psalms in general portray him not as a vindictive man, but rather as one who prayed for his enemies and sought to do them good (*e.g.* Psa. 35:13; 109:4, 5). Look at his loving response to Saul's hatred, especially the Song of the Bow, which he composed when Saul died (2 Sam. 1:17-27). Look at his treatment of rebellious Absalom and his response to his death (2 Sam. 18:32, 33). This is not a vengeful character.

(3) *God's representative and reputation*
Remember that Israel's king was God's representative, and therefore God's reputation was tied up with the king's. Offending God's anointed king was equivalent to offending God. As God's anointed king, the Psalmist was chiefly concerned with God's glory and reputation and did not cringe from praying prayers that had God's glory, not human welfare, as the ultimate end. The honour and glory of God was at stake and this was his greatest concern.

(4) *New Testament quotations*
The New Testament often refers to the imprecatory psalms. Apart from the more frequently quoted psalms of a strongly Messianic nature (Psa. 2, 22, 110, 118), the largely imprecatory Psalms 35, 69, and 109 are the next most frequently quoted psalms in the New Testament, and they are quoted, including the imprecatory verses, without any reserve, embarrassment, or qualification.

(5) *New Testament imprecations*
The New Testament also contains its own imprecations. See the 'Seven Woes' Christ pronounced on the Jewish religious leaders in Matthew 23:13-29. These were not angry

outbursts of impatient frustration but loving warnings to repent before they were overtaken by these just, divine curses. The apostle Paul also frequently prays divine curses on the enemies of the gospel (Gal. 1:8, 9; 5:11, 12; 2 Tim. 4:14; 1 Cor. 16:22). There isn't as much contrast between the two Testaments as is often thought.

(6) *Prayers for justice*

The imprecatory psalms are basically prayers for divine justice on evildoers and vindication for the innocent righteous, a theme also found in the New Testament (Luke 18:1-8). The foundation of biblical justice was retribution: an eye for an eye, a tooth for a tooth, etc. Perhaps the modern loss of this biblical view of justice is one of the reasons why so many choke on the imprecatory psalms.

(7) *Your kingdom come*

The imprecations reflect the zeal of God's people for the kingdom of God and their passionate hatred of sin and evil. Imprecation is implied even in the prayer, 'Your kingdom come,' because God's kingdom comes by defeating and destroying competing kingdoms. Anyone who loves the kingdom of God will hate the kingdom of Satan and desire its divine destruction. Real compassion for the wronged can only exist alongside indignation against wrongdoing (Matt. 23:13, 14). Both are beautiful qualities in God's sight, which he rewards with fuller measures of his Holy Spirit (Heb. 1:9).

(8) *Vengeance belongs to God*

Eighth, vengeance belongs to God. An imprecation is a prayer for God to take vengeance. The psalmist does not take vengeance himself but turns it over to God. He is effectively saying, 'Vengeance is not mine but yours, O Lord.' Carnal and worldly measures are rejected, as he fights spiritual battles with spiritual weapons (Eph. 6:12), including the 'weapon' of the imprecatory psalms. Many Western Christians seem to have lost this sense of 'being at war.' Persecuted Christians have it; and they also have no difficulty singing the imprecatory psalms.

In the late 1980s, I had the privilege of ministering to Romanian Christians who were fleeing to Hungary to escape President Ceauşescu's persecution. At the time I was struggling with the imprecatory psalms and asked a few of the Romanians what they thought. They looked at me with puzzled expressions and told me that the Romanian Christians sang the imprecatory psalms more than any others, and they did so without any qualms or questions! This also reminds us that imprecations should be reserved for the worst of God's enemies.

(9) *Save by judging*

Ninth, the call for judgment can include the desire for salvation. An imprecatory prayer will often have the good of the sinner at its heart, because we know that God will often use judgments to bring sinners to himself. This is summed up in the psalmist's petition, 'Fill their faces with shame; that they may seek your name, O Lord' (Psa. 83:16). It is exemplified in Nebuchadnezzar's conversion after being judged by God (Dan. 4), and in how God's judgment upon Elymas the sorcerer led to the salvation of Sergius Paulus (Acts 13:9-12). Thus, a prayer for judgment can co-exist with a desire for someone's salvation. We are saying, 'Lord, please judge your enemies so that they may turn to you.' We can love their souls while at the same time praying that God would defeat their persecution of God's people. We can bless our enemies, do good to them, and pray for their good (Matt. 5:44), while at the same time praying for God to punish their great evil. We can be a blessing to them on a personal level instead of cursing them (Rom. 12:14), while praying for God's vengeance if they do not repent (Rom. 12:17-21). This is a fine line to walk without sinning, as David himself recognized (Psa. 139:21-24).

(10) *Christ the curse-bearer*

Finally, and most importantly, the imprecatory psalms point us to Christ. When God's people sing these psalms we are reminded that we deserved such divine curses, that we were only spared them because Christ became a curse for us (Gal. 3:13). Also, Christ's approval of such prayers is evidenced by similar prayers being uttered now in his heavenly presence (Rev. 6:10) and heaven rejoicing over his judgment of his enemies (Rev. 16:5, 6; 18:20). These prayers for the vindication of right and the punishment of the wicked will be finally fulfilled when Christ returns for the final judgment.

I hope I have persuaded you that these psalms are consistent with the Christian gospel and can be sung by Christians, even if their solemnity causes us to only whisper them. I'm not saying they will ever be easy to sing, partly because it is difficult to explain everything and answer every objection. Much faith in God's word is required as we sing them.

12

Adding the Psalms

I hope I've given you enough good reasons to add the Psalms to your Christian diet. So let me give you some practical advice on how to actually do this in your personal devotions, in family worship, and in our congregational singing. There are some practical areas that we have already covered (like 'Praying the Psalms'), and there's one we will look at in more detail in the next and final chapter ('Analyzing the Psalms'), so I'll just touch on other areas of practical application here.

Add them to your personal devotions

The place to start is in your own private worship of God, your quiet time. There's no point in trying to persuade others to add the Psalms to their lives until you have been persuaded and practiced it yourself.

Psalms and Proverbs

Not long after I became a Christian, I heard an experienced pastor recommend that in addition to what Christians usually read from their Bibles in their daily devotions, they should consider adding some verses from the Psalms and Proverbs. The former stimulated worship and the latter stimulated practice. I decided to start this, and found that the worshipful focus of the Psalms really warmed up my heart and put me in a good spirit for my devotional time. It also got me familiar with the Psalms over some years.

Sing the Psalms

Another modification of the experienced pastor's advice was that I decided not just to read the Psalms but to sing them. They were designed for singing and therefore will produce most spiritual benefit when sung. Now, I'm not advocating that you bring the house down at 6 a.m. as you start your devotions with a musical rendition of Psalm 119. But you can sing a few verses very quietly in a private place.

That brings us to the question of which psalter to use? Obviously, the prose versions of the English psalms in our Bibles have not been versified for singing. However, there are a number of psalters available that present all or most of the Psalms in singable form. I was raised using the 1650 Scottish Psalter in our church, Sunday School, and home. Many of these psalms are now in my memory and many more have been associated in my mind and heart with spiritually transformative times in my life and that of my family.

However, while I am familiar with the words and metres, I realize that its having been composed hundreds of years ago means that some of the older vocabulary, syntax, and versification are an additional, unnecessary barrier to adoption by Christians who are not used to them. But there are many other modern psalters available which have been produced by various churches, some of which I'll highlight in the resource list at the end of this book. Most of these are faithful translations of the original Hebrew and many of them have been set to tunes that are easier for modern audiences to pick up. So there are no excuses now! I frequently use modern psalters in my own devotions as I find the new translations make me think afresh about words that had perhaps become too familiar to me.

Listen to the Psalms

I realize it's difficult to learn new songs, especially if we are older. Thankfully, most of the churches that have produced psalters have also produced resources like CDs and mp3s to help us learn how to sing them. The one I'm using right now is *The Book of Psalms for Worship*, published just a few years ago by the Reformed Presbyterian Church of North America. They have a website, Psalter.org, which contains mp3 files of all the tunes that accompany these psalms. I often play the tune as I try to sing along with the words, and usually within a couple of verses, I'm able to think more on the words than the tune. This psalter is especially helpful because it uses a lot of existing psalm and hymn tunes that are better known.

There are many Christian choirs, groups, and individual singers who have also produced CDs and downloadable mp3s of various psalm arrangements. Again, I'll list some of these in the resources at the back of the book. Some of them will suit your taste and tradition better than others. I usually sample the music before I buy it for myself. Or I will watch YouTube videos, which often have the lyrics displayed underneath. Just enter a psalm number on the search box and see what a smorgasbord of choices comes up. I'm sure you will find a genre of psalm-singing some-where that will suit your background, tradition, culture, and preferences. And from time to time, why not venture forth and explore others? I'm often surprised by the spiritual benefit of listening to other musical approaches to the Psalms, even if I still return to my trusty old 1650 Psalter.

Use a Study Bible

Most commentaries on the Psalms are too long and too detailed to read in daily devotions. I've found study Bibles have about the right length of explanation while still com-municating what is important. They also help greatly in understanding the structure of the psalm and how to divide it up if we are only reading or singing a few verses every day. The ones I've found most helpful are the *Reformation Study Bible* by R. C. Sproul's Ligonier Ministries, the *ESV Study Bible* by Crossway, and the *Reformation Heritage Study Bible* by Reformation Heritage Books. They also show how to sing the Psalms in a more Christ-centred way.

Use a daily devotional

Once you have got used to working your way through the Psalms regularly, you might want to slow down and think about the Psalms more deeply. So, from time to time, I will add a daily devotional on the Psalms to my worship. There are many different kinds of these by many different authors in many different formats (see the resource list). The one I'm about to start using is Tim Keller's *Songs of Jesus: A Year of Daily Devotions in the Psalms*. I wouldn't recommend that you start your exploration of the Psalms with a devotional. It takes too long, they don't cover all of the verses or all of the psalms, and they take away some of the benefit of direct contact with the text of Scripture and wrestling through it with God's help. However, they can be helpful refreshers now and again.

Adding the Psalms to family worship

As the Psalms were really meant to be sung with others, why not include them in the times of worship you have with your family? Some of what was said for adding them to individual worship applies to family worship too. But let me add the following.

Explain the why

If you've never sung psalms before, you probably need to explain why you want to start doing so. I hope some of the material in this book has provided you with some convincing arguments. But the two most important are that, first, this is the only songbook we know was inspired by God from beginning to end; and, second, these psalms can be sung in a Christ-centred way. See especially chapter 2 above on 'Christ in the Psalms' and the next chapter on

'Analyzing the Psalms.' One other 'plus' is that familiarity with the Psalms will hugely help understanding of the New Testament, especially the Jewish culture Jesus was brought up in, and the books of Hebrews and Revelation.

Explain the words

As some of the Old Testament language and concepts will need some explanation, you may need to prepare with a little personal study before beginning this in your family. Look for things that may not be easy to understand and use commentaries if necessary to explain. Again, the study Bibles are often the most efficient way of doing this, and the *Reformation Heritage Study Bible* has the added advantage of providing questions and points of application for family worship.

Play the music

Very few of us have the ability to quickly pick up new tunes, much less to teach them to others. Therefore, why not play a CD or mp3 before or along with your singing? It can be wonderfully inspiring to add your voice to a massed choir of angelic singers. And if your family is musically minded, you can always learn the parts to the Psalms. The Psalter. org website provides playable files of the different bass, alto, and tenor parts that can be learned and gradually meshed together. Some of the most beautiful singing I've ever heard has been congregations full of families that have learned how to sing the Psalms in four-part harmony.

Adding the Psalms to congregational singing

Again, many of the ideas outlined above can be translated to a more corporate setting, but I'd add the following advice for churches specifically, and especially to those who have responsibility for sung worship. This might also apply to youth fellowships and Bible study groups.

Go slowly

People will be at least unsettled, and probably worse, if we just stop singing all the songs they have been used to and begin singing only the Psalms. Far better to introduce them slowly and carefully. Perhaps have one a Sunday to begin with. Use psalms that are more familiar to people (*e.g.* Psa. 23; 100; 121), or use tunes that are familiar to people. If the psalm or tune is not well-known, then have it a few weeks in a row to practice until it becomes more comfortable. Perhaps adult Sunday School or other informal venues might be good venues for a core of the congregation at least to learn the psalms before they are introduced to the congregation.

Explain

We don't want to just start something without explaining the reason for it. Pick out a few of the points from this book to lay the foundation for including psalms in public worship. You will want to especially emphasize divine inspiration, the focus on Christ, the public worship purpose that is stated at the beginning of many psalms, and the communal and corporate nature of the content. Perhaps also remind people of church history and that the exclusion of psalms from public worship is a relatively recent development.

Preach the Psalms

One of the most effective ways to introduce psalm-singing is to read a psalm, preach from it, and then sing a version of it. It will then be much more meaningful to people and it will give opportunity to highlight how they can be read and sung from a Christian perspective. Quite a few churches I've preached in read a psalm in one service every Sunday, the minister adds just a few minutes of explanation, and then the psalm is sung by the congregation. Thus, the teaching content of the church service is enhanced and the sermon supplemented. Even in churches where psalm-singing is a long tradition, a few words of explanation before singing a psalm can bring it alive again for those who have grown too used to them.

Invite a choir

In Scotland, we used to have psalmody recitals, where trained and practiced choirs of psalm-singers would sing a selection of old and new psalms to various congregations. Hearing the Psalms sung so well by so many was always inspirational, and you could hear the improved singing in church the following Sunday. In Grand Rapids, we have frequent opportunities to hear the best Dutch Reformed choirs sing the Psalms in various settings. Maybe you can start a similar group to help promote and improve psalm-singing, or perhaps you can invite a choir to come and give your singing a boost both in the short- and long-term.

In some ways, each of these 'additions' to personal devotions, to family worship, and to congregational life should feed and encourage each other, and therefore will have a multiplying effect and hopefully a sanctifying effect too.

13

Analyzing the Psalms

In this chapter I want to get you started on how to benefit from the Psalms by using a simple five-step method to analyze each psalm. This will produce five practical results for each psalm: a title, a theme, a structure, lessons about Christ, and lessons about his people. I'll explain how to go about this using Psalm 1, and then give you some additional examples.

First, the *title* is the overall message of the psalm in a few words. You could think of it as the sermon title if you were going to preach the psalm, or the lesson title if you were teaching it to a Sunday School class. I usually read through the whole psalm and ask myself, 'What is this all about?' or 'How would I summarize this psalm in a few catchy words?' I've called Psalm 1 'The Great Divide' because it is all about the massive difference between the godly and the ungodly in character and destiny.

Second, the *theme* is the one-sentence statement that sums up what God is teaching in this psalm. It is specific to that psalm and not easily used to explain any other psalm.

When I'm composing the theme, I'm asking myself, 'What is the unique message of this psalm? When God inspired this psalm, what was the one major lesson he wanted us to learn?' There are many lessons we can learn from different parts of the first psalm, but what's the lesson of the whole psalm in one sentence? Here's what I came up with: 'God will make the present spiritual division permanent.'

Third, structuring the psalm divides it into maybe three or more different parts, and attempts to provide a simple outline of the main points and ideally even the sub-points. When I do this, I'm looking for major changes in the psalm. I'm asking, 'When does the psalmist change subjects, or change moods, or change perspective?' Sometimes this is really easy to figure out; sometimes it takes a bit more time; but with practice you will become faster at it. Once you identify the main parts of the psalm, you then try to find a heading that sums up the verses in each part. For example, in Psalm 1 below, the main parts are:

I. The Wise Man

II. The Foolish Man

III. The All-Knowing God

The inclusion of sub-points under each main heading comes later.

Fourth, ask yourself how the psalm is fulfilled in *Christ*. If you go through the sample outlines, and see how I've done this, you will get a feel for it. In our example, I've suggested the psalm reveals and points to Christ in these ways:

• As wisdom incarnate, as *the* wise man, he has all the wise man's characteristics.

• As judge, he will punish the wicked.

• He is the all-knowing God who will keep the righteous.

Notice how each of the three points relates to the three points of the structure. That won't always work, but it does in this case.

That leads us on to the fifth stage of analysis, which is lessons for *the Christian* from this psalm.

Once you've got the title, theme, and structure, discovering the fulfilment in Christ and the lessons for the Christian should be relatively easy.

I offer you these five analytical tools to help you think seriously and carefully about the Psalms and thereby get the maximum benefit out of them for yourself and any others you might teach. Over time, this will become an instinct or a habit that will yield much spiritual fruit in your life and the lives of others. Look through these examples with your Bible open at the psalms below and try to figure out how I came to these conclusions. You may be able to find better themes, outlines, etc. That's fine! The main aim of this exercise is to slow us down and make us think through the Psalms in a systematic and profitable way.

Psalm 1

1. Title	The Great Divide
2. Theme	God will make the present spiritual division permanent.
3. Structure	**I. The Wise Man (1-3)**
	A. He lives a separated life (1)
	B. He loves the word of God (2)
	C. He's like a fruitful evergreen tree (3)
	II. The Foolish Man (4, 5)
	A. He's like the wind-blown chaff (4)
	B. He's legless in judgment (5a)
	C. He's left out of God's family (5b)
	III. The All-Knowing God (6)
	A. He knows how to keep the wise (6a)
	B. He knows how to destroy the foolish (6b)
4. Christ	As wisdom incarnate, as *the* wise man, he has all the wise man's characteristics.
	As judge, he will punish the wicked.
	He is the all-knowing God who will keep the righteous.
5. Christians	We are daily called to follow wisdom.
	We are daily called to flee folly.
	We are promised eternal wisdom.

Psalm 2

1. Title	The First World War
2. Theme	The Lord offers peace to his enemies before he defeats them.
3. Structure	**I. The Lord has multiple enemies (1-3)**

I. The Lord has multiple enemies (1-3)

A. Multiple enemies (1, 2b)

    1. The nations rage against him (1a)

    2. The peoples plot against him (1b)

    3. The kings stand against him (2a)

    4. The rulers conspire against him (2b)

B. One aim: Destroy the Lord's lordship (2c, 3)

II. The Lord will defeat his enemies (4-9)

A. His defence (4-6)

    1. He sits in heaven (4a)

    2. He scorns their weakness (4b)

    3. He speaks of his King (5, 6)

B. His decree (7, 8)

    1. The parties of the decree (7)

    2. The promise of the decree (8)

C. Their defeat (9)

III. The Lord offers peace to his enemies (10-12)

A. Be wise citizens (10)

B. Be reverent servants (11)

C. Be loving sons (12a)

D. Be blessed refuge-takers (12c)

4. Christ	Christ is the Lord's Anointed (2), King (6), Son (7), Judge (8-12)
	See Matt. 3:17; 17:5; Acts 4:25-27; 13:33; Rom. 1:14; Heb. 1:5; 5:5.
5. Christians	Remember what you once were (1-3).
	Trust God's sovereignty in the face of persecution (4-9; Acts 4:12).
	Take the Lord's terms of peace and offer them to others (10-12).

Psalm 3

1. Title	Getting from panic to peace
2. Theme	Prayer changes panic to praise-filled peace.
3. Structure	**I. Panic (1, 2)**
	A. My enemies are many (1)
	B. My enemies are murderous (2)
	II. Prayer (3, 4)
	A. You look after me (3a)
	B. You lift me up (3b)
	C. You listen to me (4)
	III. Peace (5-7)
	A. The Lord gives peaceful sleep (5)
	B. The Lord removes paralyzing fear (6)
	C. The Lord stimulates confident petitions (7a)
	D. The Lord inspires a hope-filled future (7b)

IV. Praise (8)

A. Praise the Lord for his sovereign salvation (8a)

B. Praise the Lord for his particular blessings (8b)

4. Christ	Christ experienced the downs (Heb. 5:7) and ups (Matt. 11:25) of this psalm many times.
5. Christians	Christians panic from time to time.
	Christians are provided with a route out of that panic and towards peace.
	God saves with a sovereign salvation and blesses his people particularly.

Psalm 4

1. Title	Prayerfulness produces usefulness
2. Theme	Communion with the Lord produces concern for the ungodly.
3. Structure	**I. Communion with the Lord (1)**

A. Hear my prayer in righteousness (1a)

B. You heard me before and relieved me (1b)

C. Hear my prayer in grace (1c)

II. Concern for the Ungodly (2-5)

A. Their sin (2)

1. They exchange God's honour for shame (2a)

2. They exchange God's truth for lies (2b)

	B. The solution (3-7)
	1. Calm down (4a)
	2. Look within (4b)
	3. Offer sacrifices (5a)
	4. Trust in the Lord (5b)
	5. Seek God's favour (6)
	6. Pursue spiritual joy (7)
	7. Enjoy peace with God (8)
4. Christ	This really explains Christ's motivation and message—communion with his Father produced compassion for the ungodly.
5. Christians	Genuine concern for the ungodly flows from communion with the Lord.
	The genuine message of grace flows from communion with the Lord.

Psalm 5

1. Title	The believer's love-life
2. Theme	The believer has a passionate God-centred love-life.
3. Structure	**I. I love God's fellowship (1-3)**
	II. I love God's holiness (4-6)
	III. I love God's worship (7)
	IV. I love God's paths (8)
	V. I love God's truth (9)
	VI. I love God's justice (10)
	VII. I love God's people (11)
	VIII. I love God's blessing (12a)
	IX. I love God's protection (12b)

4. Christ	Christ had all these characteristics in perfect proportion and balance
5. Christians	The Christian strives for all these characteristics but fails, confesses, and looks to Christ … strives, fails, etc. …

Psalm 6

1. Title	Faith in the midst of forsakenness
2. Theme	The 'deserted' believer does not desert God.
3. Structure	**I. The Lord is angry with me (1-3)**
	A. The Lord is angry (1)
	B. I'm in agony (2, 3)
	II. The Lord is away from me (4-7)
	A. God's walked out (4, 5)
	B. I'm weary (6a)
	C. I'm weeping (6b)
	D. I'm weakening (7)
	III. The Lord will answer me (8-10)
	A. The Lord will answer (8, 9)
	B. My enemies will be ashamed (10)
4. Christ	Christ knew the forsakenness and faith of this prayer.
5. Christians	The Christian can feel forsaken and abandoned by God.
	A sense of spiritual desertion is the Christian's deepest sorrow.
	The Christian hangs on to his 'absent' God with faith and hope.

Psalm 7

1. Title	Divine Justice: Your treasure or your terror?
2. Theme	God's justice is a source of encouragement to the believer and terror to the wicked.
3. Structure	**I. A Just God and a Saviour (1-10)**
	A. Save me to ensure my survival (1, 2)
	B. Save me to prove my innocence (3-5)
	C. Save me to encourage your people (6, 7)
	D. Save me to vindicate my integrity (8-10)
	II. A Just God and a Punisher (11-17)
	A. God is preparing judgment for the wicked (11-13)
	B. The wicked are preparing judgment for themselves (14-16)
	C. God's justice will magnify his name (17)
4. Christ	What an encouraging prayer for Christ in the midst of his unjust personal sufferings.
	What a terrifying prayer for Christ in the midst of his just substitutionary sufferings.
5. Christians	The Christian can pray for God's just salvation.
	The Christian can thank God that Christ has suffered God's just punishment for him.

Psalm 8

1. Title	The Highest uses the lowest
2. Theme	The Lord is to be praised for using the lowest to accomplish the highest purposes.
3. Structure	**I. The exalted Lord chooses little children to win his wars (1, 2)**

I. The exalted Lord chooses little children to win his wars (1, 2)

A. The Lord is exalted above the heavens (1)

B. The Lord uses little children to defeat his enemies (2)

II. The exalted Lord chooses weak men to manage his world (3-9)

A. The Lord made the world (3)

B. The Lord chooses weak men to manage his world (4-8)

   1. The Lord thinks upon man (4a)
   2. The Lord visits man (4b)
   3. The Lord lifts up man (5a)
   4. The Lord glorifies man (5b)
   5. The Lord rules through man (6-8)

C. The Lord is to be praised through all the world (9)

4. Christ	Both parts of this psalm were fulfilled in Christ's day (Matt. 21:6; Heb. 2:6-8; 1 Cor. 15:25-27).
5. Christians	The Christian can praise God for his creation and providence.

Above all the Christian praises God for his salvation through Christ, who wins God's wars and manages God's world perfectly.

Conclusion

Well, did I succeed? Did I overcome your objections and persuade you of the immense spiritual value of the Psalms? If I did, and you are now reading and singing them, I trust you are finding Christ in them in ways you never thought possible. I hope you're finding your worship and prayer life enriched and inspired. And you're learning a ton of theology, aren't you? No, not in dense systematic theologies, but in beautiful and imaginative paintings and poems. These lyrics and metaphors are so beautiful, accessible, and memorable, aren't they?

What do you think about the free therapy? You've learned not just how to counsel yourself, but others too! Hopefully your emotional elephants are coming more and more under the authority of God's word, and you are helping others to tame and harness their feelings too so that they express them in God-glorifying ways.

But, as you've learned, the Psalms are not just about personal spirituality and our inner lives. They also call and inspire us to witness wherever God has put us. In the process, I hope you're catching something of God's missionary spirit and becoming as evangelistic as he is in his mission to bless the world. Speaking of blessing, the Psalms have taught you what you mean when you say, 'Lord, Bless my mother ... Bless my husband ... Bless my family,' etc. You may even be cautiously praying some of the Christian curses with a Christ-like spirit.

So far, so good. You've now got the 'what?' and the 'why?' of the Psalms. But there was still the 'how' problem, wasn't there? No longer! You've been given a number of practical steps to follow to add the Psalms to your life, your family, and your church. And speaking of steps, I've outlined a five-step model to get you studying the Psalms, so that you can sing them with understanding.

I'll end where I began. Imagine how happy Jesus will be to hear the songs he wrote, sang, and released, being sung again by those he wrote them for. Let's join Jesus in singing the songs of Jesus to Jesus!

Further Reading

Where to begin

Brad Johnston, *150 Questions about the Psalter: What You Need to Know about the Songs God Wrote* (Crown & Covenant Publications, 2015)

Timothy Keller, *The Songs of Jesus* (Viking, 2015)

Michael Lefebvre, *Singing the Songs of Jesus: Revisiting the Psalms* (Christian Focus, 2011)

In more detail

Richard Belcher, *The Messiah and the Psalms: Preaching Christ from All the Psalms* (Christian Focus, 2014)

Robert Godfrey, *Learning to Love the Psalms* (Ligonier Ministries, 2017)

Mark Futato, *Interpreting the Psalms: An Exegetical Handbook* (Kregel Academic, 2007)

Joel Beeke and Anthony Salvaggio (eds), *Sing a New Song: Recovering Psalm Singing for the Twenty-First Century* (Reformation Heritage Books, 2013)

The bigger picture

Derek Kidner, *Psalms 1-72: Kidner Classic Commentaries* (IVP, 2014)

Derek Kidner, *Psalms 73-150: Kidner Classic Commentaries* (IVP, 2014)

O. Palmer Robertson, *The Flow of the Psalms: Discovering Their Structure and Theology* (Presbyterian and Reformed, 2015)

Sidney Greidanus, *Preaching Christ from Psalms: Foundations for Expository Sermons in the Christian Year* (Eerdmans, 2016)

Gordon Wenham, *The Psalter Reclaimed: Praying and Praising with the Psalms* (Crossway, 2013)

Psalters

The Book of Psalms for Worship (Crown & Covenant Publications, 2010)

The Trinity Psalter Hymnal, www.trinitypsalterhymnal.org

Scottish Metrical Psalter (1650), Scottishpsalter.com

Sing Psalms (freechurch.org/praise-resources)

The Psalter (1912) (www.praise.org.uk/hymnauthor/the-psalter-1912)

Modern Psalms

Psalms, Hymns and Spiritual Songs, vol. 1, Shane & Shane, 23 July 2021

Sing! Psalms: Ancient and Modern (Live at the Getty Worship Music Conference), Keith and Kristyn Getty, 22 Feb. 2019

Every Psalm, Poor Bishop Hooper: www.everypsalm.com/listen

Banner Mini-Guides